Elastic Morality is a timely work that takes a piercing spot light and shines it right into the middle of the cultural whirlpool of diversity that young Christians are growing up in. The book profiles an emerging generation that won't stand for insipid half truths and conservative straitjackets. Without judging or lecturing, *Elastic Morality* maps a strategy for how to engage this generation in the adventure God is calling them to.

> Andy Harrington – Youth Unlimited,
> Vancouver

The crisp, insightful survey of youth culture in *Elastic Morality* is as troubling as it is unsurprising. Many of us have seen the increasing influence of this "elasticity" impact in every nook and cranny of adolescent life over the last three decades. This book wades deeply into the world of young people, recognizing that we can't fully understand the waves and currents of their world by watching from the safety of the shoreline. The "See-Stretch-Support" paradigm provides concrete ways to respond to those who stray into spiritual danger zones.

> Duffy Robbins – Professor of Youth
> Ministry, Eastern
> University

Acceptance is neither compromise nor approval. It is simply the foundation for all productive relationships. Agreeing or disagreeing with the world in which we live is not the point. Understanding it is – if we want to effectively draw young people to the love of God. Elastic Morality is a valuable resource in understanding and reaching out to our young adults. Those working with youth and young adults need this book.

> Murray Baker – National High School Director, Inter-Varsity Christian Fellowship Canada

In order to effectively reach the emerging generation, we must first come to an understanding of who they are and what they believe. Chris, Don, and John provide us with a compelling window into who young adults are and how to best instill in them a faith that has deep and reaching consequences. I'm recommending this book to youth workers, pastors, educators, and parents!"

> Walt Mueller – Founder and President, Center for Parent/Youth Understanding

Elastic Morality is a brilliantly sharp picture of Canadian, postmodern, youth culture. Let this book be your indispensable tool for making a difference with our young adults. It is essential reading for any youth worker.

> Dave Overholt – Pastor of Church
> on the Rock and
> Department head of
> Youth and Family at
> Tyndale Seminary

We've never had this research before. It's like having a new window into the hearts and minds of today's young people. For those of us who deeply desire to intentionally support today's young adults as they move toward living a tangible faith, this book is an invaluable resource."

> Iona Snair – Associate Director: YFC
> Lifeteams: School of
> Youth Outreach

Elastic Morality is a portrait of a generation painted from a palette of values unlike that of previous generations. It articulates a moral trajectory that is taking young adults of today into places their parents and grandparents would find unfamiliar. The book provides a lens through which thoughtful readers are invited into the heart of what drives 20-somethings today. So if you are a parent, pastor, educator, mentor, coach or an employer and wondered how 21st century young adults are wired, this book is for you.

> Marv Penner – Youth Specialties
> and Allaboutyouth

"This documentation of relativistic values and expressions of faith among youth leaders is essential reading for those who value effective ministry. *Elastic Morality* offers a tough dose of reality. But the authors passionately and creatively reflect on responses to find solutions that preserve the integrity of Christian faith."

> Reginald W. Bibby – Department
> of Sociology,
> University of
> Lethbridge

ELASTIC MORALITY

Leading Young Adults in Our Age of Acceptance

**Chris Tompkins, Don Posterski
&
John McAuley**

WestBow
PRESS
A DIVISION OF THOMAS NELSON

WestBow Press books may be ordered through booksellers or by contacting:

WestBow Press
A Division of Thomas Nelson
1663 Liberty Drive
Bloomington, IN 47403
www.westbowpress.com
1-(866) 928-1240

ISBN: 978-1-4497-2892-2 (sc)
ISBN: 978-1-4497-2891-5 (e)

Library of Congress Control Number: 2011918121

WestBow Press rev. date: 10/14/2011

*Grant that I may not so much
seek to be understood
as to understand.*

Prayer of St. Francis of Assisi

Chris Tompkins – team leader, youth expert

Chris serves as Managing Director of Muskoka Woods where he leads a team of 300 high school and college aged staff each summer. He recently co-authored the published research findings of "What's Happening: The state of youth ministry in Canada."  His current role and expertise generates a demand for him to speak to teens and consult with adult youth workers.

Don Posterski – author, researcher, cultural strategist

Don is a nationally acknowledged researcher and author who has devoted his career to interpreting social trends and their religious implications. Utilizing research data, Don has written and co-authored several influential books connecting the gospel with youth culture.

John McAuley – visionary, speaker, coach

John is the visionary President and CEO of Muskoka Woods – a Christian youth resort in Canada. He also serves as a member of the Arrow Leadership faculty and a lead facilitator of The Leadership Studio at Muskoka Woods. An adult learner,  John recently augmented his credentials in Organizational Leadership by completing his certification as an Adler Trained Coach.

Acknowledgements

Project Coordinator
Jennifer Anne Dumaran

Editor and Writer
Brenda Melles

Visuals
Dave White

Visionary Founders of Muskoka Woods
John and Marie Boddy

Contents

Preface

Is it possible that releasing a book into the marketplace can feel like giving a good gift to friends and vocational colleagues? For the three of us who have invested ourselves in this *Elastic Morality* project – that's how it feels. And – we like that...

One of the central findings of *Elastic Morality* contends that the power of acceptance is the primary cultural driver for today's young adults. This conclusion affirms the respected work of United States researcher, Christian Smith. The citation from Smith's book, *Souls in Transition,* mirrors the Canadian context.

> Emerging adults generally outshine their elders in being open to and usually accepting of people and lifestyles that are different from them and theirs. For most of their lives, from preschool on, most emerging adults have been taught by multiple institutions to celebrate diversity, to be inclusive of difference, to overcome racial divides, to embrace multiculturalism, to avoid being narrowly judgmental toward others who are out of the ordinary.[1]

[1] Smith, Christian and Patricia Snell. *Souls in Transition.* New York: Oxford University Press, 2009. 80.

We also want to acknowledge author Kenda Creasy Dean for coining the image of "consequential faith."[2] For Dean, it is "faith that matters enough to issue in a distinctive identity and way of life." For the *Elastic Morality* project, the image translates into the aspiration that results in robust faith – a faith that anchors the younger generation in the essence of biblical faith.

The other person who we want to acknowledge is Brenda Melles. As the editor and writer, Brenda did more than put wrapping paper on this gift. She deleted what we didn't need, weaved together our differences and crafted a coherent style into the final form.

In research projects, the make-up of the sample is always critical. In the *Elastic Morality* case, the criteria are clear. The sample is primarily Canadian young adults. In the summer of 2010 they comprised the staff of Muskoka Woods – a Christian youth camp/resort. A small sector come from the United States, United Kingdom, New Zealand and Australia. The Christian scope is ecumenical. Evangelicals represent the majority. A total of 80% come from Christian families and are churched. The same 80% continue to attend church. More than 50% have had no prior staff experience with Muskoka Woods prior to their participation in the survey. They have been screened for their Christian commitment. The conclusion: the sample represents the finest group of Christian young

---

[2]   Dean, Kenda Creasy. *Almost Christian: What the Faith of our Teenagers is Telling the American Church.* New York: Oxford University Press, 2010. 22.

adults produced by the Christian church and Canada's Christian families.

In addition, we have a second research data set gathered in the summer of 2011. The demographics are similar and the primary results are mirror reflections of the previous year. The faith of today's young adults is not a mirror reflection of the generation who preceded them.

Still – the intuitive test of research conclusions comes from those who read and ponder the results – does the data ring right? Is acceptance the primary cultural driver of today's young adults? Have these same young people gravitated to a softer and gentler set of beliefs than the older generation who walked before them? Are they content with more mystery and less certainty – more diversity and less cultural uniformity? You decide...

We don't always agree with our younger generation but we do believe in them. As we contrast some of our views with theirs, we're not sure we've always got it right. We wonder if we bundled too much bible, too much theology, too much doctrine, too much truth that required too much belief – even more belief than God ever had in mind.

Our response is not to send out the truth squad to screen the heresy out of the faith facts. Our intent is not to get it all right and then inject our certainty into the spirits of the young adults we believe in. Rather, we want to relate to our younger friends with trust and vision. The last chapter captures what we want to see more of – more beauty in our broken world.

We want to see "more living that is outward-looking, more courage to defend virtue, more generosity to counter inequity, more creativity to birth the unknown, more intellectual reflection to discern the best, more mission that pursues what is good, right and true, more living that reaches beyond-the-self – more demonstration of the essence of faith."

Chris Tompkins,
Don Posterski
and
John McAuley

Introduction

We have a story to tell.

It's a story of a group of young adults in Canada. Most have grown up in the Christian church, and most still attend. Their church attendance is spread out across a wide spectrum of denominations. They are evangelicals, Catholics, mainliners, and all the in-betweens that don't fit the defined categories.

These young adults have deep beliefs. They are genuinely seeking God and trying to figure out a way to live out their Christian faith in their everyday lives. They are serious about faith and serious about serving God.

They have great confidence in the success of their futures, and they already name themselves leaders.

In fact, these young people represent the best of what Canada has to offer as a picture of committed Christian young adults.

And yet, they are living Christian faith in a world that previous generations could never have imagined. Their world is marked by pluralism, globalization, relativism, consumerism, and technological innovation.

The world these young adults have inherited has a huge impact on what they believe and how they behave. They think and feel differently than most of their parents and youth leaders did and do.

Today's young adults are willing to stretch how they personally believe and behave in order to accommodate the differences of others. For them, it is far more important to accept others than to agree with them.

This disposition of acceptance has been drilled into them. Consequently, they welcome diversity and scorn judgment.

This book is the story of these young adults and how leaders can inspire them to live lives of consequential faith.

How can we help young adults be confident and courageous in their faith?

How can we respect differences and give space, while at the same time remaining true to what we believe?

How can we support young adults to practice the way of Jesus within postmodern cultures?

How can we lead and influence young adults without damaging what is most important to them—their relationships?

For we are God's masterpiece, created in Christ for good works, which God prepared beforehand, that we should walk in them.

- Ephesians 2:10 (ESV & NLT)

We begin our story in the context of God's big story.

We are God's art form, created in Christ Jesus for good works—designed to be a living exhibition of life with God. We are ...

- born to be creative

- made to live in Christ, embracing consequential faith

- meant to nurture a conscience with convictions, in step with God's design

- created to be a living exhibition of life with God

We are all a work in progress. We are spiritually unfinished—but created, designed, born to be a living example of God's love.

We tell our story based on evidence from a survey of 230 young adults.

We sent the survey electronically to all seasonal staff hired in summer 2010 to work at Muskoka Woods, a Christian youth resort.

Most staff came from the greater Toronto area of southern Ontario. Some travelled from as far as British Columbia and Canada's East Coast. A handful came from further afield—the United States, United Kingdom, New Zealand, and Australia.

A quarter were high school students between the ages of fifteen and seventeen.

Three quarters were in the college or university age group, between the ages of eighteen and twenty-five.

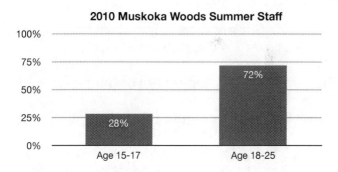

The gender split was 57 percent female and 43 percent male.

Almost everyone was either a student or working part-time.

More than half had never had any previous experience with Muskoka Woods.

The majority of our surveyed group of young adults grew up going to church.

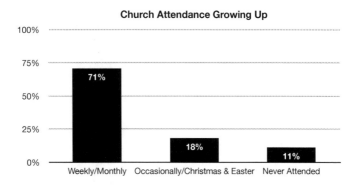

About 70 percent attended church weekly or monthly.

Almost 20 percent were occasional attendees or went at times like Christmas and Easter.

The remaining 11 percent never attended.

About 80 percent of them still go to church now.

Most of them (56 percent) go to an evangelical church like Baptist, Pentecostal, Alliance, or Community churches.

Ten percent are Catholic.

The remainder (13 percent) are mainline, like Anglican, Presbyterian, and United.

Elastic Morality **xxvii**

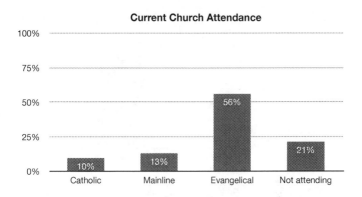

Current Church Attendance

Some of the young adults who responded to our survey don't attend church—about 20 percent.

But remember, national research in Canada tells us that only 20 percent of young adults attend services weekly or more.[3]

The national norm for young adults is 20 percent at church and 80 percent out.

Our survey results are 80 percent at church and 20 percent out.

[3]   Bibby, Reginald W. *The Emerging Millennials.* Lethbridge: Project Canada Books, 2009. 78.

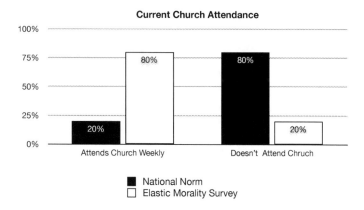

Current Church Attendance

■ National Norm
☐ Elastic Morality Survey

The group of young adults we surveyed represents a group of committed young Christian adults. They take their faith seriously, and we need to listen to their voices carefully.

What do they have to say?

Part I

How do young adults perceive their world?

Chapter 1

The Only World They
Have Ever Known

The younger generation did not create their world.

They inherited it.

They are not responsible for things we may bemoan in our culture, such as the decline in religion or the obsession with material possessions or the sex saturation of our times.

They were born into it.

It's the only world they have ever known.

What does the world look like through their eyes?

Every day, we all taste the impact of broad cultural trends in our daily lives.

Profound cultural trends like accelerating technology and materialism are not just abstract concepts. These trends march into our living rooms, our spending patterns, and our own hearts. We are not separate from strong cultural currents. They swirl around us and even within us.

The macro invades the micro.

For example, a billion books have now been sold in electronic formats. According to Amazon, Kindle e-books now outsell hardcover books. Nine out of ten youth workers now use Facebook and other social media sites to communicate with the young people they supervise.

Why?

Because rapidly evolving technology hasn't just arrived in the theoretical world. It's been around long enough to invade all of our micro worlds.

The same can be said of other broad cultural trends like pluralism and relativism.

The macro invades the micro. This is the air we breathe.

What are the most significant macro-cultural trends for today's young adults, and what do they mean for the way young adults see the world?

Young adults who were born in the late 1980s or 1990s woke up to a world that looked like this.

Diversity— a huge buffet of options

The world of today's young adults is multi-every-thing. They can choose from a huge buffet of

- lifestyle choices
- family models
- religious expressions
- church affiliations
- career paths
- educational options and
- moral practices.

Young adults rarely view only one legitimate way to live a healthy, happy, full life. There are many ways.

We call this macro-cultural trend **pluralism.**

> "What I enjoy most about the time I live in is how free it is. People are able to do anything they want and be anything they want."
>
> **—Elastic Morality Survey Respondent**

Personal choice—it's all relative

Today's young adults place extremely high value on their freedom to choose for themselves what they want off the buffet of options.

Not only that, they live in a culture where the dominant view is that the "right" choice is all relative to personal experience, personal convictions and personal opinion.

In the view of the majority of today's young adults, what is right is a matter of personal preference. Further, what is right for me is not necessarily right for you—and that's okay.

Of course, what I choose might have negative consequences for me. But ultimately, it's up to me to decide for myself.

> For most of Canada's young adults (64 percent, according to a recent representative nationwide survey), what's right and wrong is a matter of personal opinion.[4]

We call this macro-cultural trend **relativism**.

---

4   Bibby, Reginald W. *The Emerging Millennials.* Lethbridge: Project Canada Books, 2009. 9.

The shorthand label for the broad cultural trends of our time is *postmodernism*.

Postmodernism is a broad set of ideas that grew from modernism.

Both modernism and postmodernism are cultural movements that touch many dimensions of life, including music, art, architecture, literature, politics, and religion.

Modernism was the dominant way of our world in the late nineteenth and early twentieth centuries. Postmodernism is the way of our world right now.

For the church, modernism was a movement that tried to reconcile historical Christianity with the findings of modern science and philosophy. Our ideas about God and truth had to fit with our times.

Modernism was also largely about order and rationality. **In modernism, belief systems or ideologies (for example, democracy or Christianity) each had a "grand narrative"—a big story that the culture told itself about its practices or beliefs.**

In postmodernism, by contrast, any grand narrative that makes sense of the world is under suspicion. **Objective truth doesn't exist, and trying to create one big, ordered story masks all of the diversity and contradictions in any experience.**

In postmodernism, "reality" is a social construction or invention, made up by subjective self-experience. It changes with time and place and from person to person. Your reality is different from mine, and each of our realities is valid.

Today's young adults look at the world through postmodern eyes.

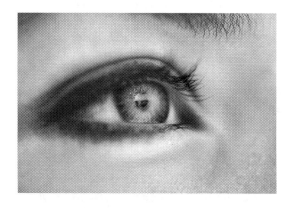

Our description of the world that today's young adults live in wouldn't be complete without sketching two more major markers.

Technological innovation is their norm.

Today's young adults were born into the information age. When they first entered the iTunes world, many had never handled a music CD, let alone a cassette tape or vinyl record. In their lifetimes, they've already moved from television to YouTube to video streaming.

They engage effortlessly with new technology. Its primary use? To stay connected and drive them deeper into their personal relationships. And no country's border is an obstacle.

Mass consumerism is the way of their world.

Today's young adults enter the world of mass consumerism the moment they exit the womb and use their first baby shower gifts. Consumerism is the way of their world, and acquiring more and better things is a virtually uncontested goal for their lives.

Christian Smith, author of *Souls in Transition,* writes:

> Voices critical of mass consumerism, materialistic values, or the environmental or social costs of a consumerdriven economy were nearly nonexistent among emerging adults … [T]he consensus position of emerging adults is this: As long as people can afford it, they may buy and consume whatever they happen to want without limit. It is completely up to them as individuals.[5]

> "I have become numb to the suffering in the world around me because I have been sucked into the North American materialistic, comfortable, independent, selfish way of life."
> **—Elastic Morality Survey Respondent**

This is the world that today's young adults have inherited.

---

5   Smith, Christian and Patricia Snell. *Souls in Transition*. New York: Oxford University Press, 2009. 67.

Pluralism is assumed, rationality is distrusted, and objectivity is unobtainable. Subjectivity is embraced, and truth is undervalued. Preference is principle, and principle is preference. Technology is fluid, and material consumption is one of life's greatest aims.

It is this world that young adults must scramble and stumble through as they try to grow up and into a life of consequential faith.

Interact

Review this description of the world that young adults have inherited. How much does this description match the views of young adults with whom you work? How much does it match your own views?

What strikes you as most significant about this inheritance? What concerns you?

How might appreciating this inheritance change the way that you engage with young adults?

Name two things that you'd like to do differently in your work with young adults in light of these reflections.

Part II

Sketching the Values and Behaviours of Young Adults

Chapter 2

Elastic Morality and the Power of Acceptance

The vast majority of today's young adults believe that it is far more important to accept others than to agree with them.

They live by the maxim of "both-and," not "either-or." In their view, championing one choice as superior to another smacks of arrogance. Instead, they are willing to accept multiple choices as legitimate.

This generation of young adults is willing to stretch what they believe and how they behave to accommodate others.

We call it elastic morality.

> **E.las.tic Mo.ral.i.ty:** An emerging Christian mindset for right and wrong that ...
> - ✓ Creates space for diversity
> - ✓ Resists judgment
> - ✓ Extends uncensored acceptance
> - ✓ Exchanges certainty for mystery
> - ✓ Stretches the boundaries of belief and behaviour

What can we learn from young adults about the virtues and vulnerabilities of acceptance?

accept

agree

No matter what

the age,
the gender,
the frequency of church attendance,

nine out of ten of the young adults we surveyed answered that accepting people is more important than agreeing with them.

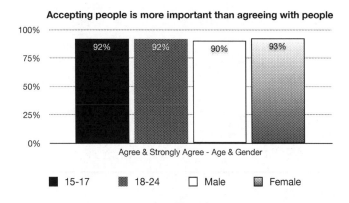

Accepting people is more important than agreeing with people

Agree & Strongly Agree - Age & Gender

■ 15-17   ▨ 18-24   □ Male   ▨ Female

"I struggle a lot with being judgmental with my fellow Christian brothers and sisters. I gotta tell you, though, it grinds my gears ... People are "God this, God that" during the summer, and then I look at their Facebook throughout the year and it's "Beer pong this, party that." It really frustrates me! I hate when people act like chameleons! However, that is also my struggle. I also gotta remember how sinful and disobedient I am as well, and to stay humble and not look down. I also struggle with battling my own flesh and temptation. So the hardest part is about living the Christian faith is, as Michael Jackson puts it, dealing with the man in the mirror first."

—Elastic Morality Survey Respondent

Young adults who do not attend church are even more likely to say that acceptance is more important than agreement (100 percent), while young adults who attend an evangelical church are slightly less likely to respond that way (88 percent).

Accepting people is more important than agreeing with people

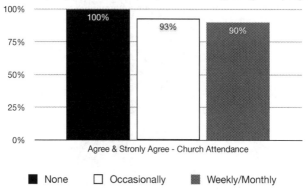

Agree & Stronly Agree - Church Attendance

■ None   □ Occasionally   ▦ Weekly/Monthly

Accepting people is more important than agreeing with people

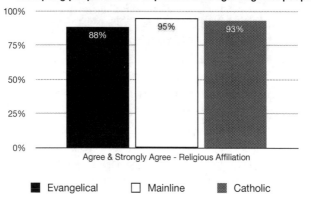

Agree & Strongly Agree - Religious Affiliation

■ Evangelical   □ Mainline   ▦ Catholic

However, despite these marginal differences in church affiliation, the findings of our research shout out that, for young adults, acceptance is their primary driver.

Trend	**Young adults are high on inclusion, and low on exclusion**
Consequence	**Diversity is divine Judgment is scorned Uncensored acceptance has the final word**

When acceptance is the name of the game, there is an open-armed embrace of all things.

Whether it is beliefs, behavioural choices, or moral issues, the predominant response of young adults is to create space for difference, resist judgment, and extend acceptance.

> "Being a Christian means treating others the way you wish to be treated, being kind and considerate to others and not being judgmental. It means being the best person you can possibly be while valuing family, friends, and privileges. It means valuing what others offer and learning from each other. It also means appreciating everyone regardless of their differences and loving one another for who we are as individuals. God made us each individuals, and we have to learn to trust that He created us that way for a reason."
>
> **—Elastic Morality Survey Respondent**

Those who draw lines in the sand risk social isolation.

Inclusion is in. Exclusion is out.

What have we learned about young adults and the rippling power of acceptance?

Acceptance is built on level ground rather than hierarchy

If the primary driver of acceptance is to have its reign, the social landscape between us has to be more like the Canadian prairies than the Rockies. Acceptance of others assumes that you are standing on level ground alongside others. One view is not necessarily higher or better than another. Instead, a broad diversity of valid views is possible.

Acceptance assumes an open system rather than a closed system

Acceptance depends on our readiness to learn from the experience and views of others. Our system of beliefs and behaviours must be open, not closed. Our relational door must be receptive to reality beyond our own perceptions. We don't need to hurry to manufacture "made-up" minds. We are ready to listen and learn from others without judgment and maybe even to shift and change our own views.

Acceptance champions a "both/and" rather than an "either/or" framework

"Either/or" people compare others with themselves. They are predisposed to affirm people who agree with them and keep others with whom they disagree at a distance. "Both/and" people grant others space to be who they choose to be. Agreement or disagreement is not the issue. "Both/and" people take permission to be who they are and give other people the prerogative to do the same.

Acceptance promotes subjectivity while demoting objectivity.

When acceptance is the name of the game, no single objective truth or grand narrative can be claimed as the measuring stick for all others. Instead, the moral pull of acceptance is to look inside for guidance. External authority is secondary. Certainty is unnecessary, and mystery is welcome. As a reference point, truth can be sidelined—maybe even put on life support.

> "I feel that I can be swayed by many different beliefs, and it is hard to know yourself and through that, know what you as a person wholly and totally believe in. There are parallel sayings between Buddha and Jesus, and there are similar teachings among all religions that encourage proper morals, but when does an individual choose, depending on their own self, what is true and right for them to believe?"
>
> **—Elastic Morality Survey Respondent**

Acceptance is fueled by compassion.

The posture of acceptance is to extend open arms to others. Empathy is a pre-condition for welcoming new relationships. Compassion is the conviction in the driver's seat. Accommodating the views and choices of others is the outcome.

Acceptance illuminates a generation gap.

Today's young adults have grown up in a post-modern world, ruled by pluralism and relativism. While the current generation of young adults drive towards acceptance and inclusion, the older generation is more likely to push for agreement and exclusion for differing views.

Christian Smith expands on this idea:

> Emerging adults generally outshine their elders in being open to and usually accepting of people and lifestyles that are different from them and theirs. For most of their lives, from preschool on, most emerging adults have been taught by multiple institutions to celebrate diversity, to be inclusive of difference, to overcome racial divides, to embrace multiculturalism, to avoid being narrowly judgmental toward others who are out of the ordinary.[6]

---

6   Smith, Christian and Patricia Snell. *Souls in Transition.* New York: Oxford University Press, 2009. 80.

Still—acceptance is not necessarily approval

Acceptance, at its best, should not be confused with either agreement or approval. Ask any parent if accepting their children is the same as agreeing with their views or approving their behaviour. The answer is obvious.

The stance of acceptance is to believe in people—without the necessity of agreeing with their views or approving their behaviours.

To do otherwise would trample on their divine and human rights.

Still—if the power of acceptance counters the courage to openly disagree or to risk social isolation—then the silence may signal approval.

The resolve is to be neither permissive with oneself nor judgmental of others.

The virtue of acceptance is accompanied with consequential vulnerabilities.

> Does acceptance make young adults vulnerable to compromise?
>
> Does it dull conviction?
>
> Does it encourage silence?
>
> Does it open space for dialogue?
>
> Does it celebrate God's beautifully diverse creation?
>
> Does it model Jesus' command not to judge other people, not to throw the first stone?

With all its virtues and vulnerabilities, today's young adults ardently embrace acceptance as their primary value.

They are highly welcoming and accepting of a diverse set of viewpoints. Further, they are hesitant to get into disagreements with others and avoid declaring one particular idea or behaviour as the only legitimate option.

In short, they operate with an elastic morality mindset that will stretch how they personally believe and behave in order to accommodate the differences of others.

Interact

Review this chapter's insights on the value of acceptance for today's young adults. On a spectrum of *agree* to *accept,* where do you sit? Where do most of the young people you work with sit?

In your experience, what are the most significant virtues of acceptance as a primary way of operating? What are the vulnerabilities?

Read this short case study of a youth leader working in a small urban church in Toronto. What might she do differently in order help young people dialogue about matters of faith while staying true to their own beliefs?

When I first started work as a church youth pastor in an ethnically diverse area of Toronto, about ten youth attended weekly programs. Most commuted in from some distance to participate. Early on in my tenure, our vision evolved to positively impact the local community. My title was changed from youth pastor to community youth worker. I started volunteering in the local junior high school. Almost overnight, the make-up of youth group changed significantly. Youth from the church families were mixing with those from the neighborhood. Christianity became the minority religion. The ethnic makeup was as diverse as the United Nations. Socioeconomic status was varied also. The youth were proud of the diversity. Muslims, Hindus, atheists, and Christians were attending youth group every Thursday night. Cultures were colliding right in our church basement.

The youth came and stayed for a variety of reasons. But there was one common theme: everyone felt welcomed, and many mentioned they felt "accepted" at the church. When the conversation turned to issues of faith, those who did not profess a Christian faith were eager to debate the finer points of Christianity. Questions like, "Well that might be okay for you to believe, but why should I?" or "Do you really believe that people with different beliefs won't be in heaven?" were often asked.

The Christian youth were hesitant to share their beliefs in Bible study time and often went quiet. The value of acceptance enabled an amazingly diverse group to enjoy being together. But when it came to conversations about faith, the dialogue stalled. You could tell that no one wanted to appear to label or judge another youth member. Instead, many of the young people chose silence.

Given these reflections, name one thing you might do differently in your work with young adults in the next six months.

Chapter 3

Resisting Judgment:
Young Adults and Sexuality

Moral decisions are traditionally framed as good or bad, right or wrong, filled with virtue or filled with vice.

However, the prevailing postmodern culture means, in the eyes of young adults, no one choice is considered the "right" choice for all times, all places, and all people. Instead, multiple choices are available, and multiple choices are valid.

Moral decisions are made in private and are a matter of personal opinion.

You may not choose what I choose, but I still accept you and respect your choice. It's not necessarily wrong. It's just not right for me.

The power of acceptance ripples out to moral issues.

Yet, church affiliation and attendance do make a difference for how young adults respond to moral questions. And they are open to conversation.

What do we have to say, and are we listening?

Young adults have different views on moral questions about sexuality and sexual behaviours than their parents and many of their youth leaders.

They have grown up in a different world.

> The average age of first marriage in Canada has steadily climbed over the past century and is now thirty-one for men and twenty-eight for women. That's five years higher than it was in 1973.[7]

> Common-law unions are growing significantly in Canada, especially among young adults. Just over one in five adults aged twenty-five to twenty-nine are in a common-law union.[8]

> In 2005, Canada became the third country in the world to legalize same-sex marriage. The 2006 Canadian census was the first to count same-sex couples. There were 45,300, of which 16.5 percent were married.[9] This number will almost certainly grow in the coming years.

---

[7]   Statistics Canada. *The Daily,* Wednesday, January 17, 2007. Marriages. *http://www.statcan.gc.ca/daily-quotidien/070117/dq070117a-eng.htm.* Accessed April 18, 2011.

[8]   2006 Census: Family portrait: Continuity and change in Canadian families and households in 2006: Findings *http://www12.statcan.ca/census-recensement/2006/as-sa/97-553/index-eng.cfm?CFID=3672469&CFTOKEN=29071597.* Accessed April 18, 2011.

[9]   Ibid.

Family norms and the sexual context of today's young adults are different from the former generation.

Today's young adults marry later and are likely to live together first. And in the eyes of the majority of young adults in Canada, same-sex marriage is not only legal, it is legitimate.

We gave the 230 young adults we surveyed a series of statements about moral issues with a focus on sexuality and asked them to respond on a scale from *strongly agree* to *strongly disagree*.

What stuck out?

One in three believes sex before marriage is okay.

Just over half believe living together before marriage is acceptable.

About half are as supportive of committed same sex-relationships as of opposite-sex relationships.

About 40 percent believe that abortion is a decision for a mother and her doctor.

Young adults also express strong views about sex in the online electronic world.

Online sexual encounters outside of marriage are seen as unacceptable by the vast majority (94 percent).

Almost a third believe viewing pornography that does not portray children is a matter of personal choice.

We analyzed all the responses according to age group and gender.

On most issues, these differences were marginal. Some notable ones are highlighted below. The older cohort (18–24) was slightly less likely to agree with the statements, with responses roughly 8–9 percent lower.

Here are the detailed questions and numbers.

	Strongly agree or agree (percent, entire sample)
Having sex before marriage is all right if you take proper precautions.	32
Decisions about having an abortion should be left to the mother and her doctor.	41
A committed same-sex relationship is as valid as a committed heterosexual relationship.	47 (female 53, male 35)
In my opinion, living together before getting married is acceptable.	51
In my opinion, having online sexual encounters outside of marriage is more acceptable than having actual physical encounters.	6 (male 12, female 2)

	Strongly agree or agree (percent, entire sample)
Viewing pornography that does not portray children is a matter of personal choice for adults.	28

Do church attendance and church affiliation make a difference as to how young adults responded to these questions?

Yes.

Church attendance while growing up tends to create more conservative views on sexual morality issues, particularly for weekly or monthly attenders.

Our data shows that occasional or seldom church-attenders have even more permissive views than those with no church attendance growing up.

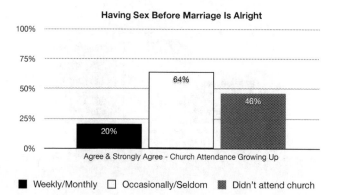

Having Sex Before Marriage Is Alright

■ Weekly/Monthly □ Occasionally/Seldom ▨ Didn't attend church

"Is it a sin to have sex before marriage? Or is it more of a guideline? It's not necessarily stated in the commandments—so is it a rule?"

—Elastic Morality Survey Respondent

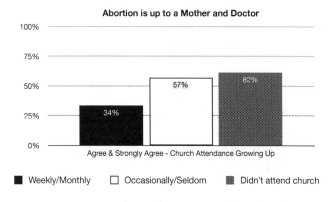

Abortion is up to a Mother and Doctor

Agree & Strongly Agree - Church Attendance Growing Up

■ Weekly/Monthly   ☐ Occasionally/Seldom   ▓ Didn't attend church

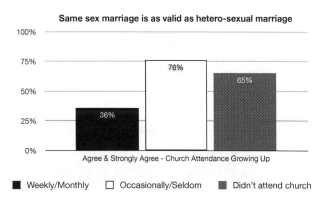

Same sex marriage is as valid as hetero-sexual marriage

Agree & Strongly Agree - Church Attendance Growing Up

■ Weekly/Monthly   ☐ Occasionally/Seldom   ▓ Didn't attend church

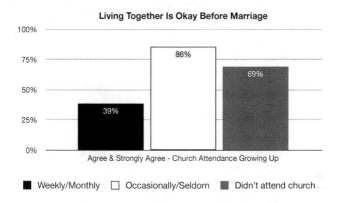

Living Together Is Okay Before Marriage

Agree & Strongly Agree - Church Attendance Growing Up

■ Weekly/Monthly □ Occasionally/Seldom ▨ Didn't attend church

Church affiliation also makes a difference with views on sexual morality issues.

Those who are affiliated with evangelical churches have the most conservative sexual moral views, with mainliners in the middle and Catholics at the other end.

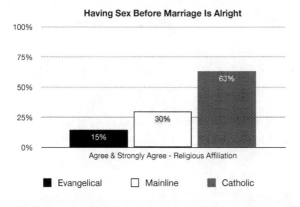

Having Sex Before Marriage Is Alright

Agree & Strongly Agree - Religious Affiliation

■ Evangelical □ Mainline ▨ Catholic

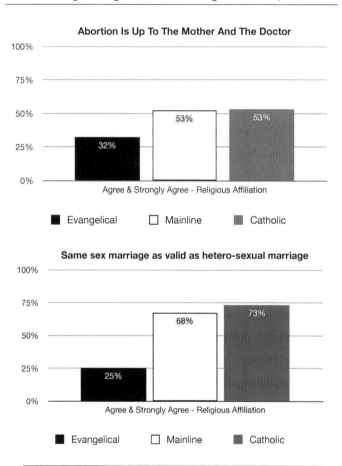

Abortion Is Up To The Mother And The Doctor

Agree & Strongly Agree - Religious Affiliation

■ Evangelical   ☐ Mainline   ▧ Catholic

Evangelical: 32%
Mainline: 53%
Catholic: 53%

Same sex marriage as valid as hetero-sexual marriage

Agree & Strongly Agree - Religious Affiliation

■ Evangelical   ☐ Mainline   ▧ Catholic

Evangelical: 25%
Mainline: 68%
Catholic: 73%

"If God created everyone, why would he create someone who is gay (known as a sinful thing in the Bible) and then they live life as someone who is seen by other Christians as a sinner? It's not a choice to be homosexual, it's who the person is, and if it's such a sin to be gay, why did God create them that way?"

—Elastic Morality Survey Respondent

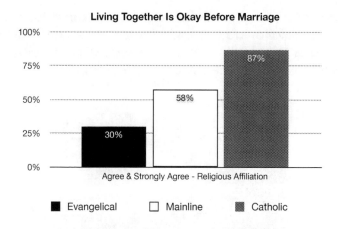

These findings on the relationship between church attendance and church affiliation and attitudes to sexual morality fit with other nationally representative research.

> "To the extent that Canadian young people are involved in religious organizations of any kind they still—at this point in history—are more likely to exhibit conservative sexual views and behavior than others"[10]

---

[10]   Bibby, Reginald W. *The Emerging Millennials*. Lethbridge: Project Canada Books, 2009. 57.

However, despite the fact that church attendance and affiliation do influence more conservative attitudes to sexuality, there are cracks in the conservative wall when it comes to sexual morality matters.

For both the evangelical and Catholic traditions, the doctrine has been unequivocal: sex before marriage is wrong, you don't live together before you get married, pro-life is the only morally right choice, and homosexuality is against God's design.

However, although evangelical and Catholic institutions may be propagating these views, individuals are charting their own course.

For more than a quarter of the evangelical young adults in our sample, abortion is up to a mother and her doctor, same-sex marriage is valid, and living together before getting married is acceptable. These results are at least twice as high for Catholics.

In short, our data shows a significant departure from the conservative views of the institutional church.

Just because the church says it, doesn't make it so for the individual beliefs and behaviours of young adults.

Trend	**High on giving permission** **Low on taking permission to define limits**
Consequence	**Postmodernism reigns** **Morality is stretched and decided in private**

This generation of young adults is comfortable giving permission to others to make their own moral decisions based on their own subjective experience and opinion.

This is the postmodern way. Assuming one choice for all people, all situations, and all times would devalue the diversity of unique personal experience.

This generation of young adults is also hesitant to define a limit that would go beyond themselves and infringe on someone else.

When it comes to moral issues and sexuality, today's young adults are uncomfortable with statements like, "That is wrong" or "God didn't design it for this." Instead, they are more likely to say, "I am still figuring out what I think, but I am definitely not going to tell them what they should do."

Morality is stretched to make space to accommodate others.

In their view, even if you choose to believe or behave differently than me, who am I to judge and tell you that you are wrong?

Today's young adults see morality as a set of private, personal decisions that are made based on personal intuition and opinion.

These decisions are not held hostage to an external truth or an objective scorecard.

Given that our sample of young adults represents a group of committed Christian young people who are serious about serving God and living out their faith in everyday life, should we be shocked by these results?

Probably not.

Their responses reflect the cultural norms of the world they live in. The macro invades the micro.

> Are we really surprised that in a world where people do not marry until their late twenties or early thirties, young adults would be open to having sex before marriage if the proper precautions are taken?

> Is it any wonder that even for young adults who are serious about Christian faith, half believe living together before marriage is okay when according to nationally representative research, by age nineteen, about 85 percent of Canadian young adults are sexually active.[11] Approval of living together before marriage is the cultural trend, and more than three-quarters of Canadian young adults approve.[12]

> Today's young adults have grown up in a world where they have been repeatedly given the message that diversity

---

[11]   Ibid. 52.
[12]   Ibid. 146.

should be embraced and that judging others' choices is out of line. In this postmodern context, should we be astonished that young adults would consider a committed same-sex relationship to be as acceptable as one of the opposite sex?

The responses of young adults to moral questions reflect the power of acceptance for them.

> "I had a real tough time filling out Section C (morality). I had strong opinions applying them only to myself. However, I don't impose my own personal values on others ... I think this section should be applicable to the individual only, and not to others as a whole. Example: The first question should be something like, 'For me, I view sex before marriage as acceptable if the proper precautions are taken.' This way, a person can answer the questions for themselves, and not for all people."
>
> **—Elastic Morality Survey Respondent**

For this generation, the drive toward acceptance is so powerful that young adults are very hesitant to tell someone else that their moral decisions are wrong.

The power of acceptance washes over to moral decisions. Elastic morality holds sway.

Interact

Review these findings on young adults and sexuality.

What surprises you? What encourages you? What disturbs you?

How might knowledge of these trends change the way that you engage with youth?

Name two things that you'd like to do differently in your work with young adults in light of these reflections

Chapter 4

Searching for Boundaries in Uncharted Waters: Young Adults and Technology

For today's young adults, using technology is like breathing.

They have grown up digital.

Their journey with technology—including computers, the Internet, and cell phones—is off any map we have ever drawn, and the impact is unknown.

Technology is redefining the way we interact with each other. It has eroded the boundaries of anonymity and privacy.

It has also opened up exciting and meaningful connections with people and ideas the world over.

But is it too much of a good thing? Are we too focused on the screen too often? Are we losing sight of the value of genuine face-to-face relationships? Are we too exposed to content that's not good for us?

Technology issues are worth engaging with young adults.

They need leaders and advocates who understand the value of technology and can also help them recognize its limits.

But how do we set boundaries in uncharted waters?

The immersion of young people into the techno-logical world begins early.

In past generations, permission to use expensive tech-nology was extended almost exclusively to "grown-ups." Today, young children are encouraged to get their hands on electronic gadgets about as soon as they are able to grasp their first teddy bear.

Not only is the immersion in technology early, it's also expansive.

Today's North American young people are satu-rated in technology.

- Around 75 percent of twelve- to seventeen-year-olds own their own mobile phone.[13]

- Adults who text typically send and receive ten texts a day. Teens give their fingers five times more of a workout, averaging about fifty per day.[14]

- Leveraging their ability to multitask, kids (eight to eighteen years of age) cram in eleven hours of media into seven and a half hours each day.[15]

---

[13] Pew Research Center's Internet and American Life Project. *Teens and Mobile Phone Survey,* April 20, 2010. http://www.pewinternet.org/Reports/2010/Teens-and-Mobile-Phones/Chapter-1/Why-teens-do-not-currently-have-a-cell-phone.aspx. Retrieved April 18, 2011.
[14] Ibid.
[15] Kaiser Family Foundation, 2010.

Facebook now has more than 500 million active users.[16]

In all likelihood, the young adult in your life is one.

---

[16] Facebook. Pressroom Statistics. *http://www.facebook.com/ press/info.php?statistics*. Accessed April 20, 2011.

Like their peers around them, the young adults who responded to our survey are wrapped up in technology.

- 97 percent have a Facebook page, and 70 percent check it daily.

- 93 percent own a cell phone (half are smart phones).

- 80 percent say text messages are a primary way they communicate with their friends.

- 83 percent own their own computer.

- 57 percent say they spend more than one hour a day online.

They use technology for entertainment.

For example, in our sample:

- Two-thirds had watched a television show online in the previous month.

- 64 percent generally download their music rather than purchasing a CD.

But its primary use is social connection.

Young adults spend hours of their lives texting, facebooking, phoning, messaging, and e-mailing their friends.

> "What I enjoy most about my current stage of life is watching *Glee* and MTV and using BBM to chat with all my friends."
>
> **—Elastic Morality Survey Respondent**

Here's what our survey tells us about what young adults do when they have free time on their hands.

High frequency	Low frequency
Hang out with friends	Flip through a magazine
Listen to music	Play board/card games
Work out	Knit/crochet
Text	Go to the mall
Do homework	Talk on the phone
Talk to parents	Draw, paint, design
Watch TV	Read a book (males)
Facebook	
Do organized sports	
Surf the Internet	

Texting, Facebook, and surfing the Internet are all priority activities. Print media and typical leisure activities of previous generations are low on the list.

Trend	**High on electronic media, low on print**
Consequences	**Technology is redefining communication, with implications on relationships**

Today's young adults are high on electronic media and low on print. You're far more likely to witness a young adult poring over the tiny screen on their cell phone than flipping through the broad pages of a newspaper or glossy magazine.

Young adults are swimming in electronic technology. Not only is it available to them from multiple portals, it's also portable. They pick it up, put it in their pockets, and take it with them wherever they go.

And not only is it pervasive, it's intrusive. What parent or youth leader has not had a conversation with a young adult interrupted by the beep of a cell phone?

Technology can facilitate communication. It can also damage it.

Social and electronic media have broken down the walls of privacy and anonymity between us, for better and for worse. We now have easy access to a huge spectrum of information and entertainment. Not all of it is true, and not all of it is good for us.

Where are the boundaries?

How can we engage in healthy dialogue with young adults on the virtues and vulnerability of technology?

Young adults need help setting boundaries on usage.

Young adults spend an enormous amount of time with their computers and cell phones. Their devices facilitate multiple activities—finishing homework, figuring out movie times, getting directions, listening to podcasts, or checking out a new band. Access to information and friends has increased the efficiency of their daily tasks.

However, many young adults have little awareness of what level of usage is appropriate and how much time is wasted. Time online means time not spent doing something else.

Young adults need to be invited into an open, non-judgmental dialogue about how much time they are spending with technology.

Questions to explore include: What usage fits the occasion? What does cell phone etiquette look like in various contexts? When is it time to turn personal technology off?

Cell Phone Basket

At the Muskoka Woods CEO program, young people come to camp for four weeks of leadership-development training. The morning sessions involve structured teaching, often in a classroom setting. The setup of the teaching environment includes a big basket at the front for cell phones. Before the session starts, the teacher says, "Put them in!" Up march young people with Blackberries, iPhones, and cell phones in hand. They carefully put them in the basket. Every break time, the teacher says, "Okay, go get your phones." In moments, the phones are grabbed and the texting begins. The cell phone basket creates boundaries around technology without damaging relationships. Leaders are saying, "The technology is not bad. We get that you want to talk to your friends. But for this moment, we want your attention."

Young adults need dialogue on boundaries for content.

At a recent job interview, a young adult was asked, "Is there anything on your Facebook page that would be of concern to families of people you will be serving in this job?"

Facebook is the new reference. According to a recent survey, almost six out of ten employers use social networking sites to evaluate prospective candidates. More and more, recruiters search for hires via social media.[17]

Yet, many young adults post things online without considering the consequences down the line.

There are a growing number of political candidates, *American Idol* contestants, and regular college students who suffer a significant price for indiscretions posted for the world to see.

How can we help young adults be more discriminating about what they post?

Today's young adults have access to a huge range of unfiltered, uncensored content on the Internet. What are they seeing?

How can we help them be discerning about appropriate content?

---

[17] Stafford, Diane. "More recruiters search for hires via social media." *Montreal Gazette.* May 6, 2011. *http://www.montrealgazette. com/business/More+recruiters+search+hires+social+medi a/4734267/story.html#ixzz1LoXPjfu2*. Accessed May 11, 2011.

The Internet has no conscience and a limitless memory. Effective youth leaders will serve their young adults well by helping them figure out boundaries for both what they post and what they view.

Young adults need conversations on boundaries for relationships.

Young people are hungry for relationships, and technology has changed the way they build them.

Facebook has re-invented the way we use the word *friend* and perhaps even the nature of friendship itself. In his article *Shift: Breathing new life into Youth Ministry* Matt Wilkinson states that, "Identity and relationship building used to come through factors such as friendship clusters, academic and athletic achievements, economic means and even one's appearance. Today it has become more complex. What has been added into the mix is the significance of their 'online connectedness.' Facebook is the place where I create my identity and share with others who I am."[18]

Technology allows us to push the boundaries of intimacy without the awkwardness of direct contact. Young adults sometimes behave online in a way that they would never consider face to face. They may also share information online that they would not dare communicate in person.

As more relationships become virtual rather than face-to-face, young adults need leaders who can guide them in a conversation about healthy friendships.

[18] Matt Wilkinson, "Shift: Breathing New Life into Youth Ministry." *Mosaic,* spring 2011.

What practices deepen and develop friendship? What is important in a strong friendship? How does the Internet affect friendship? What boundaries will help young adults monitor their online relationships, while also contributing to their other relationships?

Young adults need leaders who model healthy technology boundaries.

To lead and influence young adults, authenticity and integrity are essential. Leaders who constantly check their Blackberries at the same time they criticize young people for their excessive use of cell phones compromise their credibility. Effective leaders need to model good boundaries on usage, content, and relationships.

On the table

A leader is organizing a busy event and needs to be available to deal with questions. Before meeting with a young adult, the leader puts his Blackberry on the table and says, "There may be a moment during this meeting when I have to check this thing. Is that okay with you?" The young person can either say, "Okay, that works for me," or, "No, I really need your attention." If it's the latter, the leader makes the needed arrangements and turns it off. Either way, the dialogue has been opened, and the leader and young adult can work through the solution together.

Technology has opened up a world where we have never voyaged before.

This is new territory.

New devices and software are released at a rapid pace. Click a button, enter an online store, download, purchase, use.

New technology is often in our hands before any conversation has even been whispered about its virtues and vulnerabilities.

Today's young adults need leaders who can engage in dialogue about technology and usage, content, and relationships. They need leaders who will walk alongside them as they search for boundaries in uncharted lands.

Interact

Recall a time when you were concerned about a young adult's use of technology. What were the issues that caused you concern?

Review this chapter's information about young adults and technology. What are the most significant implications for your work with young adults?

Read this short case study of a youth pastor in a local church who is using technology to connect with his young people—and confronting some of its challenges. How can he honour the desires of his young people to connect with him, yet still set appropriate boundaries? What advice would you give him?

Youth ministry is all about relationships. In a large church, it is challenging to keep up with everyone all the time. Technology has increased my ability to connect with students outside of youth group gatherings. Facebook and texting have enabled me to reach more students and connect with them more frequently. Technology has definitely been as asset to our ministry.

Last week, however, I realized the downside of all this "connecting." I started to notice that some students were mentioning how they had not heard back from me. Complaints about texts that had not seen any response were surfacing. Students were expecting instant responses to questions sent to me. Some correspondence was via texts. Others were e-mails. I discovered that many Facebook messages and wall posts were sitting there, ignored. Utilizing multiple forms of communication with my students had become unmanageable. I couldn't keep up with it all. How can I stay on top of all the questions, messages, or personal requests when there is so many ways students connect with me? How can I help them understand that I realistically cannot respond right away—to everyone?

Given these reflections, name what you might do differently in your work with young adults around questions of technology in the next six months.

Part III

Spiritual beliefs of young adults

Chapter 5

Comfortable with Mystery:
More Faith than Facts

Our beliefs are at the core of our identities.

They are intertwined with the way we think, the way we feel, and the way we behave.

What do young adults believe about questions of faith?

Our research clusters beliefs into three sets: bounded, centred, and centreless.

The bounded set makes multiple claims to truth with confidence about their certainty. The centred set has a place for truth at the core but also makes space for mystery and diversity. And the beliefs in the centreless set lean more toward self-selection—a kind of self-construction with no claims to objective truth for all.

Most young adults are in the centred set, and those who aren't already there are probably headed in that direction.

Today's young adults are comfortable with mystery. They embrace acceptance and endorse diversity.

As their youth pastors, youth workers, spiritual mentors and coaches, do we?

Almost three decades ago, American anthropologist Paul Hiebert proposed two different ways of looking at the category "Christian." Drawing on the discipline of mathematics, Hiebert described the Christian category as either a bounded set or a centred set.[19]

Inspired by Hiebert's work, our research clusters statements about beliefs into a three-set framework.

A. Bounded set—Beliefs in HD (high definition)

Bounded sets are created by naming multiple beliefs a person must agree with.

19   Paul G. Hiebert. "The Category 'Christian' in the Mission Task." *International Review of Mission.* Volume 72, Issue 287, 421–427, July 1983.

Just as the title implies, bounded sets have clear criteria and specific boundaries.

The central question is, are you in or are you out?

Are you a set of fresh, whole, hard, crisp, green apples? If so, you're in. But if you're some other kind of fruit or even apples of disputed varieties, you're out.

In Christian communities that act as bounded sets, required characteristics of belonging usually include adherence to lists of beliefs, doctrines, and specific theology. The list of required beliefs often extends beyond a few bullet points to pages upon pages of specific truth claims about God, Jesus, the Holy Spirit, the church, legitimate modes of baptism, ministry roles of women, the nature of the atonement, the end times, and so on. You are a valid Christian if you believe "all of the above."

But not only do bounded sets depend on adherence to specific beliefs to mark the boundaries, they also depend on required practices. You may be considered a Christian not only because you believe certain things but also because you behave certain ways—you don't drink, you don't smoke, you follow a particular dress code, you disassociate from certain types of people, your moral views are predetermined, you may even be expected to vote for a particular political party, and so on.

In bounded sets, required beliefs and practices

are in high definition—clear, sharp, indisputable, and universal. They emphasize certainty. A clear line is drawn around ultimate and objective truth.

Truth claims get operationalized within denominational structures and theological systems. Protestantism, which thrived in the bounded set culture of the Enlightenment, birthed many denominations that distinguished themselves with specific claims to truth. Today's young adults, however, have little interest in sustaining the cherished and distinctive doctrines of specific denominations.

As the detailed requirements for beliefs and practices pile up and the multiple truth claims extend to many spheres, there is less and less space for ambiguity and diversity of expression.

Accordingly, the image for a bounded set is a bowl of apples. In some Christian structures, a better image is a bushel of apples. Each of the multiple apples is whole, complete, well-defined. There is not a banana to be seen.

Bounded sets are in HD—definitive, firm, and solid throughout.

B. Centred set—Beliefs with space for mystery and diversity

Centred sets are different than bounded sets. Instead of defining the set based on adherence to an extensive collection of beliefs and practices, a centred set is defined by a smaller group of crucial beliefs at the centre.

The vital question is, are you moving toward whatever we agree is at the centre?

If we are all oriented in the same direction, even though some of us might be close to the centre and some of us might be far from it, we are still all members of the set.

In a Christian community that acts as a centred set, there are a limited but strong group of defined beliefs at the centre. However, around that limited group of beliefs, there is space for mystery, movement, and diversity.

Centre-set people freely admit that now we see through a glass darkly, and that absolute truth is not something we can fully grasp as creatures of the Creator. Faith cannot exist without mystery.

Centre-set people also are comfortable living out their at-the-centre beliefs in a variety of ways. We can all be in the same set and yet still express faith differently. There's diversity in the way we under-stand heaven and hell; the way we comprehend Jesus' life, death, and resurrection; the way we dress; the way we think about moral issues and gender roles; the way we vote and so on.

There is acceptance of a diversity of expres-sions of faith, without the necessity of approval or agreement.

Centred sets have a solid core but leave more space for ambiguity and diverse expressions.

The image for a centred set is single apple, sur-rounded by some smaller apple bits and apple-sauce in a bowl.

While bounded sets are firm and solid throughout, centred sets are hard at the centre and soft at the edges.

C. Centreless Set—Beliefs under self-construction

Everybody believes something.

The main emphasis of the centreless set is that it is up to each person to find his or her own way in terms of beliefs about God, faith, and spirituality.

The bounded set calls its members to adhere to clear statements of objective truth and clear instructions for behaviour.

The centred set calls its members to orient themselves to an agreed core of beliefs, with space for mystery and diversity.

The centreless set is more humanistic and subjective. The challenge for the centreless set is to navigate beliefs based on personal history, informed opinion, and individual preference.

For the centreless set, beliefs are under self-construction. Truth is more of an option than a reference point.

Having personal opinions and deciding what is right and wrong for yourself does not necessarily mean you are a person without principles. People can choose to construct their lives without God and still have substance and integrity. However, self-constructors do so without the trustworthiness of God's wisdom. As they become personal architects of their own lives, they live with the vulnerability of trusting themselves.

The image for the centreless set is bowl of applesauce with a few apple chunks.

Centreless sets are soft at both the centre and the edges.

Beginning from this three-pronged belief framework, we assigned belief statements into the three sets.

A. Bounded Set—Beliefs in HD	B. Centred Set—Beliefs with space for mystery and diversity	C. Centreless Set—Beliefs Under Self-Construction
What's right and wrong is clearly defined in the Bible.	What's right and wrong is informed by the Bible's teachings.	What's right and wrong is a matter of personal opinion.
Christianity is the only true and valid religion.	Christianity is the most true and valid religion.	All world religions are equally valid.
It is very important for Christians to witness to non-Christians and actively influence them to become Christians.	God wants Christians to witness to their faith, but people's decisions are really between God and themselves.	How people respond to God is a personal matter, and we should respect their privacy.
I believe that through the life, death, and resurrection of Jesus, God provides forgiveness to those who repent and confess their sins.	I believe that Jesus' life, death, and resurrection happened, but people can be forgiven without knowing about Jesus.	I believe that God is merciful and that anyone who lives a good life will have their sins forgiven.
Christian truth is pretty black-and-white. The Bible is very clear about what to believe and how to behave.	The Bible contains Christian truth, but it's often difficult to figure out what to believe and how to behave.	Figuring out what is true and what to believe and how to behave is not really possible—so I decide for myself.

Belief statements in the bounded set (A column) are the most sharply defined. Using words like "clearly," "only true and valid," "very important," "black-and-white," these belief statements emphasize certainty and absolute truth.

Belief statements that represent the centred set (B column) are more textured and less categorical. There is more space for interpretation. Several of them are framed in two parts—a core belief statement, followed by a "but," which acknowledges that the way that belief gets acted out is complex and personalized to individual experience.

Belief statements in the centreless set (C column) emphasize "personal opinion," "privacy," and deciding "for myself." There is more space for individual choice.

Using these three belief sets, we asked young adults which group best represented their personal beliefs and views.

41 percent answered A—the bounded set

40 percent answered B—the centred set

18 percent answered C—the centreless set

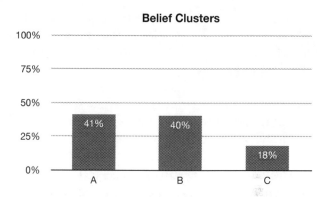

Belief Clusters

In other words, almost 60 percent of our sample—a group of young adults with a high level of commitment to Christian faith—was outside of the bounded set (A) category.

Differences between age cohorts were not significant.

Gender did make a difference for the A and B choices, with males more likely to select the A (bounded set) and females more likely to select B (centred set).

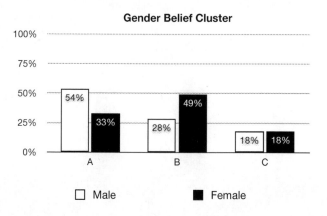

Gender Belief Cluster

☐ Male   ■ Female

Treading on the soil of gender differences is always dangerous. However, in this case, the contrast is considerable. The young men are leaning more to a closed system while the young women are more open to spiritual diversity. Here, the male bias is to draw sharper lines while the female disposition is to be more comfortable with ambiguity. Whereas young men in our survey position themselves to set up numerous "belief requirements," young women tend to respond with more compassion and grant more space for the views of others.

Of the three belief sets, which group best represents your personal beliefs and views?

When we analyse responses to the belief sets according to church affiliation, the results are both predictable and surprising.

Expectedly, evangelicals have a significant lead in the bounded set group (A) at 59 percent.

However, well over a third (37 percent) of young adults with evangelical affiliation place themselves in the centre set group (B).

Mainliners are the most evenly spread across the three sets.

Catholics are predominantly in the centred set group (B), with over a third in the centreless set (C), and a very small number in the bounded set (A).

Which group best represents your personal beliefs and views?

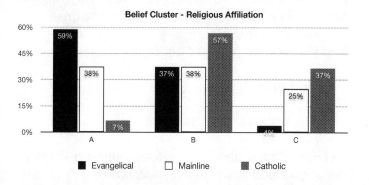

Belief Cluster - Religious Affiliation

To summarize, our research grouped belief state-ments into three different sets according to our three-pronged belief framework. Each set had a statement about right and wrong, a statement about Christianity in the context of other world religions, a statement about witness and evan-gelism, a statement about Jesus and forgiveness, and a statement about the Bible.

Our findings were that the majority of young adults were outside of the bounded set (A).

The only exception was evangelicals, but even so, 41 percent of evangelicals were outside the bounded set.

Not only did we ask young adults to identify their beliefs according to the clustered sets, we also asked them to examine their beliefs one by one. To do this, we used the same statements that made up the belief sets but asked about them in separate questions.

When we analysed the beliefs one by one in-stead of in a clustered set, were the responses still roughly 40 percent bounded (A), 40 percent cen-tred (B), and 20 percent centreless (C)?

The short answer is no.

Three significant findings stuck out.

First, on witness and evangelism, only a quarter of the young adults surveyed believed that "it is very important for Christians to witness to non-Christians

**and actively influence them to become Christians,"
while over 60 percent believed that "God wants
Christians to witness to their faith, but people's decisions are really between God and themselves.**"

The first statement (with minority support) is a clear example of bounded set
thinking. You're in or you're out, and a
central preoccupation of the insiders is
to move people across the boundary
from out to in.

The second statement (with majority
support) is an example of centred set
thinking. I have a belief that I am oriented toward, but it's up to you and
God if you want to move in that direction too.

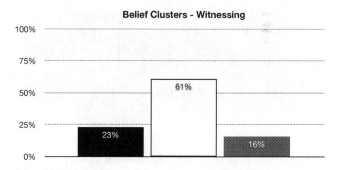

Belief Clusters - Witnessing

■ It is very important for Christians to witness to non-Christians and actively influence them to become Christians
☐ God wants Christians to witness to their faith but people's decisions are really between God and themselves
▨ How people respond to God is a personal matter and we should respect their privacy

> "The toughest part about living the Christian faith for me is witnessing to non-Christians."
>
> **—Elastic Morality Survey Respondent**

Second, views on the Bible suggest that young adults see the Bible more as an important reference than a clear authority.

A third of the young adults in the study (33 percent) believe that what's right and wrong is clearly defined in the Bible, while more than half (54 percent) say what is right and wrong is informed by the Bible's teachings.

> "How can the Bible be proven to be true if there is scientific evidence that humans evolved from primates?"
>
> **—Elastic Morality Survey Respondent**

Third, the data show that traditional views of Jesus still reign among young adults.

Over 60 percent believe that "through the life and death and resurrection of Jesus, God provides forgiveness to those who repent and confess their sins." By contrast, just over 20 percent say that "I

believe that Jesus' life, death, and resurrection happened, but people can
be forgiven without knowing about
Jesus."

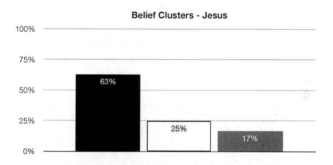

Belief Clusters - Jesus

- ■ I believe that through Jesus, God provides forgiveness to those who repent and confess their sins.
- ☐ I believe that Jesus' life, death & resurrection happened but people can be forgiven without knowing about Jesus.
- ▨ believe that God is merciful and that anyone who lives a good life will have their sins forgiven.

"At this stage of my life, one of the big
questions I have about God and the
Christian faith is, if one lives a moral and
ethical life without knowing God, will
they be saved?"
—Elastic Morality Survey Respondent

In fact, the historically orthodox views of Jesus
among young people are so high that they skew
the overall picture when we look at beliefs as a
clustered set. Without the Jesus variable, just over
half of young adults (52 percent) would fall into
the centred set.

Here's where it gets even more interesting.

When we compare the overall results on spiritual beliefs for young adults in our survey to the spiritual beliefs of a sample of youth leaders across Canada, we discover something striking.

Over the past year, we have had the opportunity to present the same clustered belief sets reported in this chapter to key adult youth leaders from across the country. In each case, we have asked the adult youth leaders to indicate which set of beliefs—bounded (A), centred (B), or centreless (C)—best represent their personal beliefs and views.

The first event was a one-day gathering of youth pastors and organizational leaders from Ontario, Quebec, and eastern Canada, called "Elastic Morality." Seventy-eight ministry leaders responded to the question.

After that, almost two hundred Christian Camping leaders from across our nation answered this question at the annual Christian Camping International conference.

Finally, fifty key denominational leaders from coast to coast participated in this part of the survey at the Canadian Youth Workers Conference in Toronto.

In total, these three events involved 317 adult ministry leaders from across our country.

We've collected the responses. The position is clear and consistent.

By a huge majority—96 percent—Christian youth leaders from across Canada personally align with a "bounded" set of beliefs.

As a reminder, here's how the results of current adult youth leaders compare to our sample of young adults.

	Adult youth leaders[20]	Young adults[21]
Bounded Set (A)	96%	41%
Centred Set (B)	4%	40%
Centreless Set (C)	0%	18%

In other words, while the majority of young adults are outside of the bounded set (A) category, the opposite is true for adults who work alongside this younger generation.

There is a clear generational divide.

---

[20] Sample size 317, from three events listed above.
[21] Sample size 230, from Elastic Morality Survey.

So—what's the conclusion? What is the trend? What are the consequences?

Trend	**High on subjectivity, low on objectivity** **High on historic orthodoxy, low on biblical authority**
Consequence	**Truth is on life support, dead for many** **Individuals hold the veto vote for what is right and wrong**

This generation's bias is to be uncomfortable with excessive certainty.

True, four out of ten place themselves in the bounded set. However, four out of ten position themselves in the centred set, and two out of ten in the centreless set.

In other words, more young adults identify themselves as out of the bounded set than in.

By contrast, the vast majority of leaders identify themselves with the bounded set. As a result, a large proportion of leaders of young adults are not in the same belief set as those they lead.

There will also always be a small group of young people who will resist the mainstream and stay in a more conservative, bounded-set understanding of Christian faith. However, because of the prevailing norms of our postmodern culture, if young adults have not already moved to a centred-set understanding of Christian faith, many of them are packing for the journey.

Given elastic morality and the power of acceptance, this is not surprising. For most young adults, objective truth is on life support. Grand statements of truth that do not allow for diversity and mystery do not resonate with this generation.

For today's young adults, uncertainty is not necessarily negative. It's okay not to know. They are more at home with the ambiguity of faith than the certainty of facts.

Interact

Consider the young adults with whom you work. How many would identify with the centred-set group of beliefs? Now, consider yourself, which belief set best represents your own personal beliefs.

Review the findings about beliefs for today's Christian young adults. What excites you? What concerns you?

Reflect on the findings highlighting the large generation gap between the beliefs of young adults versus the beliefs of their leaders. What are the implications for leading young adults when belief sets are not shared? Should leaders focus their attention on trying to move the beliefs of young adults towards the bounded set? How might young adults respond to that approach?

Given these reflections, describe what you might do differently in your work with young adults in the next six months.

Chapter 6

Orienting Young Adults towards the Essence of Faith

Faith is the confidence in what we hope for and the assurance about what we do not see.

What are we confident about, and on what are we assured?

When it comes to matters of Christian faith, the majority of today's older teens and young adults have departed from the more conservative theological views we find in the bounded set. Bounded-set beliefs draw a hard line around absolute truth and insist on adherence to an often long list of required beliefs and behaviours to belong.

Today's young adults do not buy the songs of certainty. They embrace mystery and diversity. They resist being told—or telling others—that they must express their faith in uniform and specific ways.

Yet many young adults still want to pursue a life of consequential faith.

What now?

Leaders of young adults who push for full measures of certainty risk chasing away those they want to influence. Effective youth leaders appreciate where young adults are coming from, meet them where they are, and travel with them on their journey of faith.

We can nurture today's young adults in robust faith by helping them hold to the essence of faith, rather than insisting that they adhere to a required list of expressions of faith.

Can we be centred around the essence of faith while not selling excessive certainty?

For many leaders of young adults in the Christian context, leaving behind bounded-set thinking and multiple claims to objective truth feels like selling out.

In their eyes, by not insisting that young adults buy into a particular set of right beliefs and right behaviours, they are endorsing relativism and compromising truth.

However, depending on what branch of Christian tradition you come from, the list of right beliefs and right behaviours differs. The sixteen thousand different expressions of the global Christian church have created more claims to truth than you can fit into a freight train.

> "Why do Christians have to fight among themselves and other religions about who is 'right'?"
> **—Elastic Morality Survey Respondent**

The church's long list of truth claims are organized into written confessions of faith, decrees, creeds, catechisms, and articles of religion. Some truth claims are about the time before you are born, and others are about the time after you die. Some buy into pre-millenialism, and others claim post-millenialism. Some throw their weight behind Christus Victor, and others advocate satisfaction theory. Some dress up, and some dress down.

Too often, the list of required characteristics to belong to the Christian category is so overflowing with claims to truth that humility and mystery have been quietly ushered out the back door.

Somewhere along the line, the essence of faith got mixed up with a long list of expressions of faith.

When working with young adults, many churches, parents, and youth leaders have bundled the core elements of faith inseparably with particular lifestyle choices, political views, worship styles, economic philosophies, social issues, and distinctive denominational doctrines. Then, like a product-marketing strategy, they have instructed young adults to choose and live by the whole bundle.[22]

We need to stop bundling.

We need to believe more, about less.

We need to go deeper, with fewer requirements.

We must keep deep convictions but recognize that not everything is essential.

Effective youth leaders will walk alongside young adults to help them define and hold to what is the essence of faith.

---

[22]   We are thankful to Peter Held, whose blog entry used the term "bundling" in connection with expressions of Christian faith. *http://rachelheldevans.com/doubting-children-peter-held?utm_source=feedburner&utm_medium=feed&utm_campaign=Feed%3A+RachelHeldEvans+%28Rachel+Held+Evans+-+Blog%29*. Accessed April 6, 2011.

This is a centre-set strategy—helping young adults get oriented towards a limited but strong core of beliefs. Inspiring young adults to build a robust faith means helping them move and grow towards that centre.

It's time to wrestle with the non-negotiables. What's at the centre? What's important? What is it that we can't live without? What is the content of the apple in the applesauce?

A bounded-set strategy depends on building fences to keep people in or out.

A centre-set strategy depends on digging a deep well of life-giving water to draw people to a shared and central place.

What bubbles out of the Christian well?

The essence of Christian faith grows from:

> Jesus' uniqueness

> The Bible's authority

> Identity and belonging as children of God

> Mission behavior

Jesus' Uniqueness

"In the fullness of time ..." Jesus came to life on earth in an obscure place—Nazareth. Clothed in human flesh, Jesus' historical entrance was a one-time-only event.

Fully God
       Fully human
              Prophet
                     Teacher
                            Friend
                                   Self-sacrificing Savior ...

The finest demonstration of a life ever lived.
         God's plot "to save people from their sins."

Jesus' birth, death, and resurrection.
Our reasons to believe and behave with confidence.

(Galatians 4:4; Matthew 1:21; John 1:1, 1:14; I Cor-inthians 15:3–4, 12–19 (RSV))

The Bible's Authority

At first glance, the Bible is a book of stories. The table of contents looks confusing. But it is a unique book. It is God's book. But I only get the significance of the book when I realize that God's Spirit signed my name on the cover page. The Bible is God's book given to me and given to us.

A closer look at the historical story divulges the plot. The Bible reveals how people respond to God and how God responds to people. The people players seem intent on mapping their own journey without God. They stray. They inevitably create their hell on earth.

But God is the consistent one. God knocks until there is an answer. God calls people back to their home. God reveals truth that restores. God loves the wayward into being what they are meant to be.

The Bible is God's trustworthy map. When we are wise we surrender to the authority of the map's directions.

(2 Timothy 2:15–16; Hebrews 4:12; 2 Peter1:20–21 (RSV))

Identity and Belonging

The younger generation continues to wrestle with the complexities of "Who am I?" and "Where do I belong?" On both fronts, Christians have a response.

I am a child of God.
I am marked with the images of my Creator.
I am a follower of Jesus—a disciple, a believer, a learner.
I am rescued and restored—a new person "in Christ."

I am created for community.
I'm an individual, but I don't travel solo.
I struggle to find my way alongside my spiritual family.
We worship, we study, we pray, we serve ... together.
I belong with others who share my Jesus' faith ...

Who am I? Where do I belong? I am a follower of Jesus, finding my place with other followers of Jesus.

(Genesis 1:27; John 1:19–28; 2 Corinthians 5:17–18; Romans 12:3–8; I Peter 2:9; Hebrews 10:23–25; Galatians 6:10 (RSV)

Mission Behaviour

Over time, various denominations and church traditions have generated a myriad of mission maps.

Many have a single focus on evangelism—the personal salvation of the lost: Great Commission (Matthew 28:18–20).

> Others give priority to love—loving God, self, and neighbour: Great Command (Luke 10:25–28).

> > Some put their emphasis on social justice—concern for the poor and oppressed: Great Requirement (Micah 6:8).

> > > Many lift up the need to love your neighbour. Mission is a ministry of reconciliation for some. Others champion the cause of world missions.

Numerous organizations are called to express their mission among specific demographics like students, recovering alcoholics, or members of other world religions.

Whatever the mission map or strategy may be, the focus is outward rather than inward. Mission behaviour counters the image that God is "on call" to meet *my* needs.

Another common denominator of mission behaviours is that they make demands on the precious currencies of time and money. Whatever the mission cause may be, involvement affects our calendars and bank accounts.

Christian living without involvement in some expression of mission is incomplete—even fraudulent. The genius of the expectation is that mission protects us from being self-absorbed or becoming so super-spiritual that we are of no earthly good.

The mission vision shared by all God's people links with Jesus' prayer we have all learned to pray together—"Thy Kingdom come on earth as it is in heaven."

(John 20:19–23; John 21:6; James 1:27; Corinthians 2:14–17; I Corinthians 15:58) (RSV)

As we continue to envision the substance of a robust faith—

As we invite young people to believe more, about less—

And as we go deeper, with a focus on fewer core beliefs—we must also remember these trends and consequences.

Trend:	**Young adults are high on un-certainty, low on certainty**
Consequence:	**Leaders who push for full measures of certainty risk chasing away those they want to influence**

Today's young adults are suspicious of excessive certainty and multiple claims to truth.

Leaders who push their young adults in that direction risk shutting down the very dialogue they want to encourage. Instead of walking alongside young adults on their journey of faith, their insistence on a long list of requirements may damage the relationship beyond repair.

To nurture a robust faith among young adults, we need to distinguish between the essence of faith[23] and the expressions of faith.

Our tendency with young adults has been to propagate a lot of things that we can live without.

We don't need more theories of faith translated as doctrinal requirements or interpreted biblical biases propagated as facts of faith. We don't need subjective declarations of truth imposed as the only truth that is really true.

---

[23]   We want to acknowledge that the "essence of faith" quadrilateral is rooted in David Bebbington's groundbreaking work: *Evangelicalism in Modern Britain: A history from the 1730s to the 1980s* (London: Unwin, Hyman, 1989).

Instead, we need effective youth leaders who are confident and assured about what is at the centre of Christian faith. Leaders who are ready to journey with young people as they discover and define that essence for themselves.

"I guess my question is, why does he allow so much crap to go on in the church? There are so many different denominations and views on Christianity; why has he allowed so much separation? I mean I get that we do have an enemy and he has to be somewhat to blame. I also understand that we are human and far from faultless. So the mixture of those two is probably catastrophic, but still I beg the question, why God? I pray that he will bring us together and help us live him out day to day, rather than argue about creation and how it happened or silly disputes over baptism. Let's just love each other and care for the broken and the needy and love God. Is that not what we're called to?"

—Elastic Morality Survey Respondent

The centred-set approach affirms vibrant faith with substance. But it still leaves space for personal reflection.

It's more open than closed.

It does not over-claim truth but humbly and ardently turns and moves towards the essence of faith:

> Jesus' uniqueness ... God with skin and bones, modeling a life of extravagant love through life, death, and resurrection.

> The Bible's authority ... God's book of stories, history, poetry, prophecy, and instruction, given to us to guide us. God's revelation to keep us on track in our journey of life.

> Identity and belonging ... God's adoption of us as treasured children, included in a diverse community, held together as a body of believers.

> Mission behavior ... God's call for us to look outwards and live life beyond ourselves, serving others.

Interact

Where have you witnessed the "bundling" of Christian faith in your own experience? What was the impact of bundling numerous expressions of faith into one package?

How do you distinguish between the essence of faith and the expressions of faith in your own life?

A centred-set strategy with young adults involves helping them define and hold to a limited but strong set of core beliefs. How might adopting a centred-set strategy change the way you work with young adults?

Given these reflections, describe what you might do differently in your work with young adults in the next six months.

Part IV

Inspiring young adults to live a life of consequential faith

Chapter 7

See: Embracing Anchored Faith

Profiling the younger generation is one thing. Figuring out how to serve them—to influence them for God and good is another matter.

As we unpack patterns of belief and behaviour for young adults, we also wonder, what do we do with the analyses? What proactive role can we play?

As leaders of young adults, we want them to live lives of consequential faith—"a faith that matters enough to issue in a distinctive identity and way of life."[24]

But how do we inspire young adults to live this faith that matters—to believe it, breathe it, and behave it?

We believe the strategic response to today's young adults is threefold[25]:

- **to see them**

---

[24]   Dean, Kenda Creasy. *Almost Christian: What the Faith of Our Teenagers Is Telling the American Church.* New York: Oxford University Press, 2010. 22.

[25]   Sinclair, M. (2011). "See, Stretch, Support: Three Powerful Conversations that Create Connections.": http://www.melindasinclair.com/see-stretch-support

- **to stretch them**

- **and to support them.**

One by one, that's what the next three chapters are about.

Seeing ... is about looking below the surface. Seeing seeks to understand and takes us deeper into the core identity and worldview of today's young adults.

The intent is not to shape and squash young adults into our ideas or frameworks but to create space for young people "as they are." Seeing young adults with grace and openness positions ourselves as leaders who can engage them and help them see themselves more clearly.

We know they live with acceptance as their watch-word. When we genuinely see young adults, accept them where they are, and give them space to grow towards what they will become, we can invite them to live out their identity as followers of Jesus, grounded in the essence of faith.

Seeing young adults means we can play a role in influencing them to embrace anchored faith.

When you look at this picture, what do you see?

Do you see an old woman?

A young woman?

The truth is, each woman, the young and the old, is represented in this illustration[26]. It is possible to look at this image and see two distinct portraits.

The diversity in our own stories shapes our view of everything we see.

You and I are not a blank slate. We are not an empty vessel. Each of us is a beautiful tapestry of

---

[26]   Boring, E. G., 1930. "A New Ambiguous Figure," <u>American Journal of Psychology</u>

backgrounds, ethnicity, family, education, hopes, fears, and dreams. Each of us is in the world with a distinct set of experiences and attitudes.

As leaders, we never come newly born and untouched to any situation—including the challenge of leading young adults.

Now, what do you see?

Good grades? College applications? Delinquency? Alcohol? Promiscuity? Entitlement? Energy? Cynicism?

Understanding our unique perspective and our tapestry of identity becomes even more significant when we focus our attention on young people. How we view someone shapes our attitudes and interactions towards them.

The lenses we use to frame today's young adults have direct implications on how we lead them.

Ephesians 2 provides a beautiful picture of God's view of young people—of all of us. Laying this picture over the lives of young adults enables us to "see" as "God sees."

> **We are God's art form ... created in Christ Jesus for good works ... which God designed for all people ... in order to be a living exhibition of life with God.**
> (Ephesians 2:10 Paraphrase)

Young adults are God's art form.

They are created in Christ Jesus.

God has breathed life into them and made something new.

The intention is that they can be a living exhibition of life with God, in both words and actions—to be the hands and feet of Christ in our world. This plan was established long before we even met them.

It is a picture of life, hope, and inspiration.

By God, in God, and for God.

When we see with God's eyes, we understand and value human life as a gift from God rather than a reward for achievement. We see the image of God in everyone. We celebrate the value of every person, whether they conform to our preferences or not.

Is this also your vision of the young adults you work with?

> *"The children now love luxury; they have bad manners, contempt for authority; they show disrespect for elders and love chatter in place of exercise. Children are now tyrants, not the servants of their households. They no longer rise when elders enter the room. They contradict their parents, chatter before company, gobble up dainties at the table, cross their legs, and tyrannize their teachers."*

The quote above is attributed to Socrates, somewhere around 400 BC. It seems there is a long tradition of adults criticizing the shortcomings of young people.

What about now? How do we see today's young people?

Let's start with how young adults *think* we view them.

"I am frustrated that there is a large part of the aging population that doesn't respect you because they judge you as a rotten teenager. They aren't willing to listen to your ideas or perspectives because they don't think you comprehend things or care about life issues."

—Elastic Morality Survey Respondent

"Adults do not fully believe in my abilities as a leader."

—Elastic Morality Survey Respondent

"My biggest frustration is being accepted for who I am by my mother. Anything I do doesn't seem to satisfy her."

—Elastic Morality Survey Respondent

Many young people feel judged by the adults in their lives.

Their perception is that far from being seen as God's art form, they are seen as inadequate and not entitled to full-fledged conversation and consideration.

Instead of being invited into lively, respectful, non-judgmental dialogue, many young people feel that they are written off if they don't fit the mold their leaders have made for them.

As we consider how we see young people, it is important to remember that young people are growing up—literally.

They are travelling through ages and stages.

Young adults live with and through multiple transitions that occur internally and simultaneously. Changes in physical, cognitive, and social development add to the pressures of the external realities of their lives.

Young adults are constantly being developmentally stretched.

"I feel God has placed me where I am for a reason, and I am no longer learning for my future, but am actually being used by God in what I love and am called to do ... I feel like in the last two years and this year, I have exploded with potential and possibilities that are starting to actually take place in my life."

—Elastic Morality Survey Respondent

Around the time of puberty, the young brain changes remarkably. The progress in cognitive development allows adolescents to think in ways not possible in childhood. It is worth highlighting five changes that occur in the minds of teenagers:[27]

---

[27]   Steinberg, Laurence, Vandell, Deborah, & Marc Bornstein. *Development: Infancy through adolescence.* Belmont: Wadsworth, 2011.

- For the first time, they can **think about possibilities**. The ability to use deductive and inductive reasoning arrives on the scene. Hypothetical thinking begins.
- Topics of love, democracy, and justice rise to the surface as they begin to **think in sophisticated ways about abstract concepts**. Brain development has increased capacity and interest to engage in topics such as politics, religion, and morality.
- They become better at **thinking about the process of thinking.** Internal reflection tempts them with self-indulgence. They can become centred on "me." This makes them susceptible to the beliefs that everyone is watching them (imaginary audience) and that their experiences are unique (personal fable). Ideas of "invincibility" set in as they are convinced they are not subject to rules that govern others.
- Improvements in the ability to **think about things from multiple vantage points** take place at the same time. They are able to put themselves in someone else's shoes for the first time.
- **Ideas or concepts become relative, rather than absolute**. Adolescents are much more likely to question others' claims and less likely to accept "facts" as absolute truths.

Ages and stages of young adults are unfurled from day to day.

When we see young adults, we recognize not only that they are travelling through ages and stages, they are also in the middle of a journey of faith development.

Generally speaking, physical, cognitive, and social development unfolds in a consistent, identifiable manner.

Faith development is the same.

According to James Fowler, our ways of understanding faith mirror our ways of knowing and valuing other aspects of life. As young adults move into their twenties, they enter a stage of faith development called individuative-reflective faith.[28]

This stage is marked by critical reflection on previously held values, beliefs, and commitments. Not only are inherited religious traditions examined, but also other faith traditions are evaluated for their merit or what they have to offer. Secular value systems and worldviews embedded in their environment are taken into consideration.

This is often a distressing process for young adults and for the adults around them who are witnessing the journey.

If the familiar practices and beliefs are not discarded, they are held firmer than before.

---

[28]   Fowler, James W. *Stages of Faith: The Psychology of Human Development and the Quest for Meaning.* New York: Harper Collins, 1981.

"I'm really starting to discover the type of person I want to be and am really trying to live my life through Jesus. I am maturing in my faith and am learning that loving others is of much higher importance than personal success. I enjoy the struggle of reminding myself daily to try to live as Jesus lived and not worry about gossiping or new clothes. I love how much I love God right now and how close I have grown with Him. I'm excited to see what happens next; He has blessed me so much and I hope I can bless others through Him at this stage in my life."

—Elastic Morality Survey Respondent

As we genuinely "see" young adults, we may recognize in them a search for *discriminated* faith and for *owned* faith.

For young people born into Christian families, one of the challenges of remaining Christian is discriminating their "family-inheritance faith" from their own.

Robust faith is not cloned faith. Robust faith is *discriminated faith*.

Beyond just reflecting and examining one's faith history, discriminated faith is also self-embraced. It has distinctive markings that are mine. It may involve beliefs, behaviors, lifestyle, and church choices that are distinct from one's family faith.

Finding discriminated faith is a faith development marker.

"What are my true personal convictions? (Not the ones I have been brought up to believe.)"
—Elastic Morality Survey Respondent

Another faith development marker for young adults results in an owned faith.[29]

---

[29]   John Westerhoff. *Will Our Children Have Faith?* New York: Seabury, 1976.

The central thrust of owned faith is that people take responsibility for their personal faith and they assimilate a Christian identity. They privately and publically claim: "I am a follower of Jesus."

The owned faith marker is an exercise of their God-given gift of freedom to accept or reject God's presence and influence in their lives.

For young adults, without the emergence of both discriminated faith and owned faith, consequential faith is out of reach.

Not only should we appreciate that young adults are stretched between ages and stages, and journeying through faith development, we should also see that young adults are defining and examining their values.

We asked the young people who responded to our survey to rank their important current values.

Do you see what we see? We see virtue in their values.

They treasure friendship, family, and forgiveness.

Honesty is held in high esteem.

Concern for others and working hard is a priority.

Spirituality and personal faith are highly affirmed

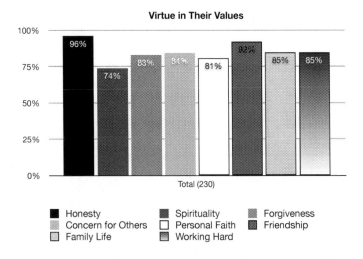

Virtue in Their Values

These values are the building blocks of a robust faith.

Not only does the value ranking identify the most important values for our sample of young adults, it also reveals what is at the bottom of the pile.

Do you see what we see? We also notice vulnerability in their values.

Intelligence has been diluted.

Creativity has diminished.

The environment often takes a back seat.

Global issues are treated with indifference.

Today's young people have inherited a multi-minded world. Before lunch they have already waded through an array of choices. Complexity has altered and impacted their attitude towards various important issues.

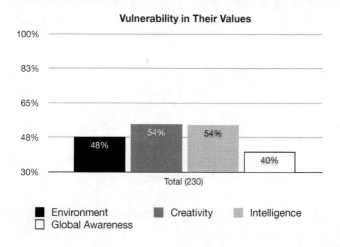

"People my age don't get me. They don't feel the same sense of urgency to change the world or even to do the right thing. Sometimes I feel like I am the only one my age who cares about world issues, or living for God, or following the law."

—Elastic Morality Survey Respondent

In summary, genuinely seeing young adults means critically examining how our unique story shapes our own perspectives.

When we view young adults through stereotypes and preconceived notions, we are in danger of missing them entirely. They will be reticent to engage in what we bring to the table. One size does not fit all.

It also means appreciating the ages and stages of young adults, their process of faith development, and the virtues and vulnerabilities of their values.

Seeing is not stereotyping. It is not judging a book by its cover. It is not looking at one static frame out of context from the whole movie. It is allowing the story to unfold and the journey to be travelled.

Finally, it means walking alongside young adults to help them see themselves.

Self-reflection and self-awareness are marks of

maturity. As leaders, we can help them awaken to this part of their journey.

What does healthy self-esteem and self-perception look like for a young adult anchored in Christian faith? It means I am a child of God, beautifully created in God's image. It means God loves me, forgives me, knows me, and has lavished me with grace. It means I have unique gifts, given by God.

It also means I am not the centre of the universe. I am called to serve others beyond myself. I am fallen and often look away from God's ways—but God always welcomes me back. I am a steward of creation. Everything I have and I am is a gift of God. I am commissioned above all else to love God and love my neighbor.

Young people will be well served when their cognitive and emotional capacity to reflect critically is not only directed to the world around them but is also focused on themselves. This generation's vulnerabilities—to be captured by culture, to be enticed to extend their dependence on parents, to protect their transparency behind technology—are addressed in part by self-awareness.

As leaders of young adults, we want to see them and give them space to be who they are. We also want to invite them to embrace anchored faith:

> — a faith that is owned and personal—their own chosen story, their own experience with God so far;

— a faith that is grounded in a small set of important essentials rather than bogged down by a long list of requirements to belong;

— a faith where they accept the differences of others, but still claim their identity as followers of Jesus and children of God;

— a faith where they give the Bible authority and live in a way that serves others.

But young people will not open the door to that dialogue until we see them without judgment, without stereotypes, and without superficiality.

When you look at the young adults in your life, what do you see?

Interact

Make a list of all the qualities, characteristics, and attitudes you think of when you consider the young adults you work with. Divide the qualities into two columns—positive and negative. What do you notice?

How closely aligned is your vision of young adults to God's vision of young adults as "God's art form, created in Christ Jesus for good works which God designed for all people in order to be a living exhibition of life with God"?

Review the information in this chapter on how we see young adults, ages and stages, faith development, and the virtues and vulnerabilities of their values. What strikes you as most significant for your ongoing work?

Describe two things you will do differently in the next six months in your work with young adults as a result of these reflections.

Chapter 8

Stretch: Expressing Courageous Faith

As leaders of young adults, we are called to **see** them deep below the surface—give them space to be who they are and invite them to embrace anchored faith.

But leaders do more than just see those they lead. They stretch them.

Stretching is about identifying and creating opportunities and challenges for young adults.

Opportunities to achieve, to excel, and to be delegated responsibilities. Opportunities to succeed.

But not just creative, positive, present-tense opportunities that stretch young adults—challenges, too. Challenges to boldly respond to what they see, to resist the ways of the world that are so enticing, and to escape the grip of cultural conformity.

In stretching young adults, we want to challenge them to

- discern what is right
- resist what is wrong, and
- dissent what is unjust.

In all this, we want to stretch them beyond self-interest, to be open and responsive to needs of the world around them.

At the heart of the matter, stretching young adults is about inspiring them to express courageous faith.

For today's young adults, there are too few anchors.

It's hard to be optimistic. The mood of the moment has punched out confidence in human progress. Too many wars ... too much unemployment ... economic meltdowns ... political back-stabbing ... fractured families ... fraudulent heroes ... unattainable university entrance test scores ... too many truth claims ... too many unreliable opinions ... too many personal insecurities.

They have inherited a heavy load.

Somehow, hundreds of Facebook friends don't seem to be enough to carry it.

Good God—are you really good?

Today's young adults grew up in postmodern times, where truth is more about opinion than fact. In the world they have inherited, the subjective triumphs the objective.

Accordingly, the moral guidance system of today's young adults primarily depends on their personal opinion and experience.

What are the consequences?

> ... [W]hen life's push comes to shove for emerging adults, such a condition thwarts many of them from ever being able to decide what they believe is really true, right and good ... Very many emerging adults simply don't know how to think about things, what is right, or what is deserving for them to devote their lives to. On such matters, they are very often simply paralyzed, wishing they could be more definite, wanting to move forward, but simply not knowing how they might possibly know anything worthy of conviction and dedication.[30]

---

30   Smith, Christian and Patricia Snell. *Souls in Transition*. New York: Oxford University Press, 2009. 293.

As leaders of young adults, we are called to walk alongside them as they seek clarity in this fuzziness, and conviction to live their lives with purpose.

We are called to invite them to experience and live out consequential faith.

When we stretch young adults, we invite them to express that distinctive, courageous faith in beliefs and behaviours.

"The most difficult but rewarding part of Christian faith is following through on the beliefs that you have and being able to stand up for God."

—Elastic Morality Survey Respondent

We stretch them by challenging them to look beyond self-interest as they hold fast to what is right, stand firm against what is wrong, and tackle injustice with all their might.

The spirit of these postmodern times is to discard the categories of "right" and "wrong" and to wash away the lines between them.

But for followers of Jesus, some things are still "right," and others are "wrong." Some attitudes and behaviours are life-givers. Other attitudes and behaviours are life-destroyers. God's genius and love for us wants to protect us from destroying ourselves and inflicting pain on others.

But another cultural and relational challenge is thinking that your beliefs are superior to others'. Claiming that your conclusions about what's true are more right than the claims of others violates the tolerance code.

So as we "work out our salvation with fear and trembling,"[31] and as we strive to lead young adults with humility and integrity, we're confronted with many questions.

> If tolerance is a cardinal virtue, how can we expect young adults to make discerning judgments?

> What are the things we stand up for? And how do we do that while respecting those who believe differently?

> Can we press young adults to be accountable to a higher standard than their own?

> How can we stretch them and inspire them to express courageous faith?

---

[31] Phillipians 2:12. (RSV)

As leaders of young adults, we challenge them to discern what is right.

To discern what is right, we look to a reliable source of Christian truth. The history, stories, poetry, and teaching of the Scriptures are our moral guidance system.

For example, the Beatitudes, as ambiguous as they may seem, are trustworthy guides to personal, relational, and social well-being. Injected with God's wisdom, they are the right way to live.

The Ten Commandments are more than good ideas. Ignore them and you will damage yourself and others. Practice them and you will serve your best interests and give gifts to others who share your life.

Living right brings forth the fruit of the spirit in us, our relationships, and our world —love, joy, peace, patience, kindness, goodness, faithfulness, gentleness, and self-control.

When we discern what is right and express it with courageous faith, we often swim against the cultural current.

> Generosity trumps greed.
> Love triumphs over selfishness.
> Honesty quashes deceit.
> Protection dwarfs exploitation.
> Self-control overshadows being undisciplined.
> Mutuality dispels isolation.
> Gratitude surpasses entitlement.

Humility shatters arrogance.
Serving others transcends discounting others.
Integrity overwhelms being unscrupulous.

As people of Christian faith, these are the things we claim to be right and true.

To young adults we say, these are the things that are worth standing up for.

Not only must we walk alongside young adults as they discern what is right. We must also lead them to resist what is wrong.

Again—there is complexity here. Just as there are shades of darkness, in moral decision-making, there are ranges of consequences.

Not all bad choices are equally destructive. Some indiscretions are more consequential than others. The damage of some sin is internal. It is housed in secrecy and remains as personal property. Other sins reach out and wreak havoc on relationships. They can destroy families and ruin organizational life.

The implications of some bad-choice behaviours take time to concoct their misery. The outcomes are like committing suicide in slow motion. Other behaviours hit their targets with bull's-eye impact. The damage is immediate.

So be courageous. Take time to reflect on past behaviours that went wrong for you. As you relate, teach, and mentor alongside the younger generation, encourage them to develop a radar system that alerts their conscience. Inspire them to resist what is wrong.

The list of wrongs below is not ranked in order of importance or meant to be comprehensive. It is illustrative. But be aware—

Refusing to forgive ...
  is wrong
Gossip and slander
Sexual unfaithfulness
Hate
Lying
Stealing
Unrestrained lust
Permissiveness
Bitterness

Selfish indulgence
Indifference
Sexual abuse
Oppression
Laziness
Manipulation of the
  vulnerable
Coveting
Mindless consumption
  ... is wrong

To young adults we say, these are some of the things that are worth standing against.

> "Overcome evil with good"
> ~ Romans 12:21 (RSV)

We also challenge young adults to dissent what is unjust.

Yes—Denounce …	Yes—Champion …
Racism	Bridge building
Apathy	Peacemaking
Stereotyping	Advocacy
Oppression	Creation care
Human trafficking	Righteous anger
Blaming the poor	Purposeful passion
Gender biases	Global awareness
Exclusion	Local awareness
Social segregation	Inclusion
Hunger	Compassion
Extreme poverty	Gender equality
Child-headed households	Freedom of religion
	Empathy
Death from curable diseases	Environmental stewardship
Government policy indifference	Informed action
	Human rights
Corruption	Protecting the vulnerable
	Value of life

Data from our survey demonstrate that young adults do maintain a sense of personal obligation to respond to the needs of people in less-developed countries.

This is an encouraging sign, and it shows the openness of young adults to respond to concerns outside their borders and to take action on global justice issues. This posture of personal obligation to people in less-developed countries is a starting point for stretching experiences and for dialogue between young adults and their leaders.

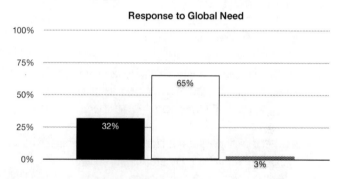

Response to Global Need

- ■ The Canadian government alone has an obligation to help provide to people in less-developed countries
- ☐ I have a personal obligation to support the governments' commitment to help provide to less-developed countries
- ▦ The Canadian government does not have an obligation to help provide to people in less-developed countries

"... Whatever is true, whatever is noble,
whatever is pure, whatever is lovely,
whatever is admirable—if anything
is excellent or praiseworthy—
think about such things."
– Philippians 4:8 (RSV)

In all of this—discerning what is right, resisting what is wrong, and dissenting what is unjust—we need to stretch young adults beyond their own self-interest.

The current critique of young adults often charges them with "entitlement"—an assumed "right" to the privileges of life, without the associated work and responsibility it takes to get them.

As Judith Warner from the *New York Times* summarizes,

> **For the past** few years, it's been open season on Generation Y — also known as the millennials, echo boomers or, less flatteringly, Generation Me…. [M]illennials, born between 1982 and 2002, have been depicted more recently by employers, professors and earnestly concerned mental-health experts as entitled whiners who have been spoiled by parents who overstoked their self-esteem, teachers who granted unde-served A's and sports coaches who bestowed trophies on any player who showed up.[32]

Where does this sense of entitlement come from? Parental over-protection, over-indulgence, and family structures that encourage extended de-

---

[32]   Judith Warner. "The Why-Worry Generation." *New York Times,* May 28, 2010. *http://www.nytimes.com/2010/05/30/ magazine/30fob-wwln-t.html*. Accessed June 1, 2011.

pendence well into adult years are probably
entitlement-inducers.

**But whatever the source, an antidote to entitle-
ment—which might also be called excessive self-
centredness—is stretching young adults beyond
self-interest with challenges and opportunities to
give beyond themselves.**

> "I met kids whose parents are in jail and
> are going through a hard time, yet they
> have such positive attitude and the
> brightest smiles I have seen in a while. It
> showed me how blessed I am, and how
> I take so many things for granted or so
> many little problems too seriously, while
> these kids have lost a lot and are still
> smiling."
> **—Elastic Morality Survey Respondent**

Today's young adults need opportunities to be
fully Christian in a world that is charging ahead
with little regard for God.

They need leaders who can help them discern
what is right, resist what is wrong, and dissent what
is unjust.

They need opportunities and challenges that
stretch them beyond self-interest.

Effective leaders stretch young adults by giving them opportunities and challenges that build their courage and confidence to stand up for what they believe and to live a life of consequential faith.

Interact

Recall a real-life experience from your past where someone gave you an opportunity or challenge that stretched you. What made that experience positive for you? Negative?

Review the content in this chapter about discerning what is right, resisting what is wrong, dissenting what is unjust, and stretching beyond self-interest. Which items on the lists are the most challenging for the young adults you work with?

Consider your work with young people in the coming six months. What specific opportunities can you create to stretch them—both in terms of positive opportunities to succeed and also challenges to express courageous faith?

Chapter 9

Support: Living Tangible Faith

Effective leaders of young adults see them for who they are and invite them to embrace anchored faith. They also stretch them with opportunities and challenges and inspire them to express courageous faith.

But leaders do more than just see and stretch young adults. They support them.

Supporting is fundamentally about encouraging young adults. It is leveraging our positive influence with them and sending "I believe in you" signals.

It is coaching and mentoring them with a personal bias that they will pursue what is best, become what God intended, and contribute what is needed in these times.

Supporting young adults means nurturing their commitment to creatively live tangible faith.

When they need help or support, today's young adults turn to people who already have significance in their lives. They draw their inspiration from individuals with whom they already have the deepest personal relationships.

Their biggest heroes are not the rich, famous, and notable. For the strong majority, their biggest heroes are their parents. Everyday experiences trump high-profile achievements.

> *"The people [teens] most admire and imitate are those with whom they maintain personal connection, friendship or interaction ... For better or worse, teens are emulating the people they know best."*[33]

We asked the young adults we surveyed to rank a list of their sources of influence. Their top answers, in order of priority, are illustrated below.

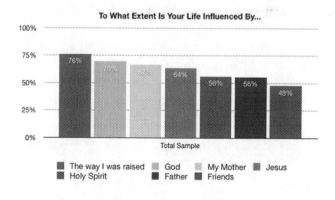

To What Extent is Your Life Influenced By...

- The way I was raised
- Holy Spirit
- God
- Father
- My Mother
- Friends
- Jesus

33   Barna Group. 2011. "Teen Role Models: Who They Are, Why They Matter." *http://www.barna.org/teens-next-gen-articles/467-teen-role-models*. Accessed June 3, 2011.

Star power may keep them tuned into their favourite movies, television shows, or music, but media ranks low on the list of influences for young adults. Celebrities, government, Facebook, and advertising also find their place in the lower tier.

Rather, young adults have a high level of openness to influence from adults they know and trust.

How then can leaders who work with young adults in the Christian context support and influence them to live lives of consequential faith?

Supporting young adults involves coaching, mentoring, modeling, and sometimes offering tangible resources.

This is a highly relational process.

The process involves walking side by side, working together, and playing together. It usually involves both structure and great flexibility.

The circumstances are situational, but young people are open to receive what they need to push past the barriers the world throws at them.

> "I'm really starting to discover the type of person I want to be and am really trying to live my life through Jesus."
>
> **—Elastic Morality Survey Respondent**

Sometimes we need someone to show us how tangible faith works itself out.

Sometimes we just need someone to listen.

Young adults crave meaningful relationships with adults they respect.

"I am still unsure about where my faith is at in my life."
—Elastic Morality Survey Respondent

How can a support model for young adults work out in practice?

Here's one example.

Several years ago, Muskoka Woods, a Christian youth resort, instituted an intentional support system to build consequential faith in the lives of young adults.

They called it a "one-on-one" coaching model.

Every young adult met weekly with a more spiritually mature (and, honestly, often only slightly more mature) peer.

It took some courage to actually believe it might work.

Thirty to sixty minutes a week one on one.

Being as open as a person is ready for.

Having at least one other person who is looking out for you.

The initiative grew from a desire that every person would have someone else to talk to—one on one. It was a tiered model that cascaded from the president to the youngest staff member. No one slipped through the cracks.

The approach was simple—conversations that involved listening and asking questions. The focus spanned how the person you were supporting was doing physically, emotionally, socially, and spiritually.

The structure was designed to ensure that a support relationship was in place and nurtured with time and mutual commitment. When questions arose, when problems escalated, or when the journey was difficult, an obvious person was there.

For some participants, it was several seasons before the coaching moved past superficial participation. Others bought in right away.

One leader cannot offer this level of support to every young person in his or her circle of influence. But they can work to ensure that each person has access to this level of care from someone.

Within those structured experiences, leaders can make appropriate theological, counseling, and leadership-training resources available.

***

The conclusion: As we support young people to face a wide variety of theological, sociological, psychological, interpersonal, and spiritual issues, intentional mentoring and coaching relationships can have profound impact.

"Sometimes, I get big ideas, but I feel trapped by my current life situation: school, homework, work, family, friends. It's a lot to keep up with while trying to live like Jesus. Our modern consumer society can be frustrating as it interferes and distracts from God's way sometimes. I also get frustrated sometimes when I worry about things in my life; I find it hard to fully trust God and trust that He will be with me and take me through my struggles."

—Elastic Morality Survey Respondent

In 2009, a group of senior-level leaders connected with Muskoka Woods conducted a major research project on the state of youth ministry in Canada.[34]

The research used four nationwide surveys—to church youth ministers, Christian youth organization youth workers, youth volunteers, and former youth workers.

One survey question was, "Did you have a formal mentoring or coaching relationship, and what did you gain?" Of the respondents, 265 answered "yes." When we analysed their responses, we discovered important insights about both the inputs and the outputs of coaching. Here's a summary.

---

[34] Don Posterski, Marv Penner, and Chris Tompkins. *What's Happening? The State of Youth Ministry in Canada.* Muskoka Woods, 2009.

What does a mentor or coach bring to the table?

Modelling	Their lives are respected
Wisdom	They have theological and cultural insight
Expertise	They have a specialized role
Spiritual Direction	They guide with honesty and maturity
Collaboration	They work *with* you and provide opportunities
Listening	There is freedom to ask questions; you feel safe
Encouragement	They affirm and acknowledge
Friendship	They are interested in you
Advocacy	They champion your best interests

For those who are mentored and coached, what are the results?

Personal confidence	Life skills and competence
Self-aware	Perspective
Challenged	Leadership lessons and skills
Supported	People skills
Affirmed	Inspiration
Accepted	Accountability
Spiritual maturity	Practical advice
Motivated	Prayer support
Nurtured gifts	Planning and goal-setting
Grounded	Knowledge from more experience

For both the person being coached and the person doing the coaching, the experience can be transformative.

Positive coaching relationships can make a life-changing difference.

As we support young adults and challenge them to live out tangible faith, we want them to:

Pursue what is best ...

> We live in a culture of choices. As young adults confront a need for direction in our multi-choice world, we want to help them adopt the mind of Christ as they discern the best direction. Paul writes in 1 Corinthians, "Everything is permissible—but not everything is beneficial. Everything is permissible—but not everything is constructive." Just because it is expedient does not mean it will edify. As leaders, we support young adults to pursue what is best.

Become what is intended ...

> We are all in a state of becoming—of growing, emerging, journeying. As we support young adults, our desire is that they will become what God intended— loving deeply, growing in faith, living outwardly, modeling God's character and concern for all of life. We know that moral discrimination is necessary to navigate in these times. Consciences with deep convictions are essential in order to express tangible faith—faith that is lived out in words and in action.

Contribute what is needed ...

We don't support young adults as an end in itself. Support is a means to equip and enable their contribution to the world. Our world is graced with beauty and scarred with brokenness. We need more beauty—more living that is outward-looking, more courage to defend virtue, more generosity to counter inequity, more creativity to birth the unknown, more intellectual reflection to discern the best, more mission that pursues what is good, right, and true, more living that reaches beyond the self—more demonstration of the essence of faith.

Young adults need our support.

They need our faith, our hope, and our love. They need leaders who will mentor and coach them, accept them, challenge them, listen to them, advocate for them, and model life in Christ for them.

In a culture that so often leans away from God, only with intentional support will they be able to live tangible faith.

Interact

Recall a real-life example from your past in which you have had a positive experience of support from an adult. What were the key factors that made that experience important for you?

Review the story of Muskoka Woods' one-to-one coaching program. How can you ensure that more people in your circle have someone who can regularly support them with time, prayer, connection, and conversation?

Consider the young adults you work with. Which ones need more support? Describe two things you can do to provide them with better support in the next six months.

Conclusion

Elastic morality.

A mindset for right and wrong that
   creates space for diversity,
        resists judgment,
             extends uncensored acceptance,
                  exchanges certainty for mystery,
                       and stretches the boundaries of
                       belief and behaviour.

The term is a portrayal of the world that today's generation of young adults has inherited—a world where pluralism, relativism, and post-modernism reign. A world where objectivity bows down to subjectivity, truth claims are looked on with skepticism, and inclusivity trumps exclusivity almost every time.

A world where a spirit of acceptance has the final word.

We know from our survey data that elastic morality has consequences for beliefs and behaviours—whether they are interpersonal, spiritual, sexual, or technological.

We also know that if we ignore these trends and consequences, we cannot hope to influence today's young adults to live lives of consequential faith.

This book is the story of a group of young adults who are serious about loving God and living the Christian faith. The majority of them are actively involved in a church and have been heavily influenced by the Christian teaching they have received in their childhood.

But they do not stand outside of the broad cultural currents, where elastic morality flourishes. They are at home there.

The majority of today's young adults have left the more conservative theological frames and beliefs that their leaders still hold to. Instead, they are trying to navigate their Christian faith in an age of acceptance where claiming "truth" and clear categories of "right" and "wrong" for all people is enough to get them socially isolated and relationally rejected.

Accordingly, today's young adults surrender to diversity and bow to mystery.

They are ready to know what they don't know.

How do we as leaders respond?

By drawing them towards the essence of faith. By dropping the long list of unnecessary required expressions of faith. By modeling acceptance and keeping the door open for dialogue. By walking alongside them in their journey of faith development.

As we see, stretch, and support young adults towards consequential faith, we can call them to:

> **Anchored faith** ... where I claim my identity as a follower of Jesus, grounded in the essence of faith.

> **Courageous faith** ... where I passionately and graciously stand up for what really matters, where I carry a conscience with conviction, and I am not afraid to live against the cultural current.

> **Tangible faith** ... where I demonstrate my faith in words and action, with love for God and neighbour that is more self-giving than self-serving.

As leaders of young adults, we connect with them at one of the most turbulent stages of their life.

As their bodies and brains are developing and changing, so too are their beliefs, attitudes, and behaviours. They are walking—sometimes running—through a journey of growth and maturity. Along the way, they encounter choices, opportunities, success, and celebration—and also challenges, complexity, failure, and regrets.

As we journey with them, we must strive to see them below the surface, to stretch them with opportunities that extend them beyond themselves, and to support them with prayer, insight, and encouragement.

As we seek to influence them, we invite them to be their very best.

Along the way, they will sometimes disappoint us and discourage us. But if we keep our eyes open to see as God sees, they will also reveal and demonstrate to us God's character and action in ways we never expected.

Some art masterpieces were never finished: Mozart's *Requiem,* a heartbreaking piece of music. Coleridge's "Kubla Khan," one of the world's most famous poems. Gaudi's Sagrada Familia, a stunning feat of architecture.

So it is with young adults.

They are God's art form. They are in Christ but not complete.

Any great story has a great ending. But their story is still being told, and we get to play a role.

We are all and always still unfinished.

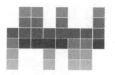

THE LEADERSHIP STUDIO
AT MUSKOKA WOODS

A place where people learn to look at their world and say,
"It doesn't have to be this way"... and do something about it!

The Leadership Studio set in the beauty of Muskoka on Lake Rosseau, Ontario, Canada. A unique place where –

- Experiential programs challenge your group in leadership and team building

- Skilled staff facilitate your planning

- Access to on site leadership resources motivates your innovation

- The environment stimulates you and your staff to dream and achieve

- Interactive learning inspires leaders to change their world

The Leadership Studio where – creativity reigns, friendships flourish and confidence grows

For more information check out
www.theleadershipstudio.ca